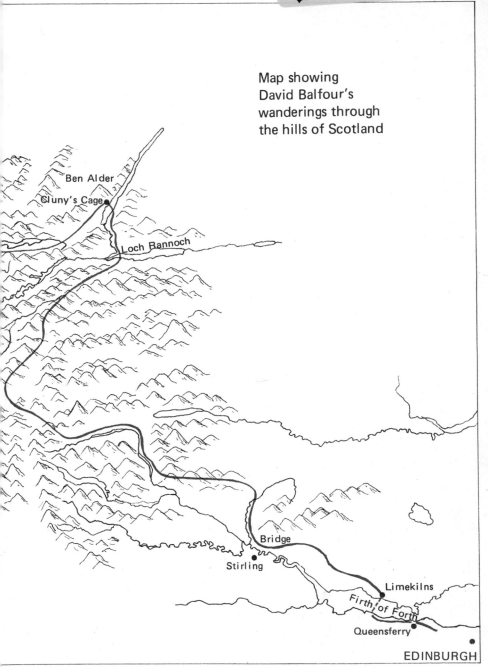

Map showing
David Balfour's
wanderings through
the hills of Scotland

Ben Alder

Cluny's Cage

Loch Rannoch

Bridge

Stirling

Limekilns

Firth of Forth

Queensferry

EDINBURGH

OXFORD PROGRESSIVE ENGLISH READERS

*General Editor: D. H. Howe*

# Kidnapped

# Kidnapped

## by R. L. STEVENSON

HONG KONG

OXFORD UNIVERSITY PRESS 1976

KUALA LUMPUR SINGAPORE JAKARTA TOKYO

*Oxford University Press*

OXFORD LONDON GLASGOW NEW YORK
TORONTO MELBOURNE WELLINGTON CAPE TOWN
IBADAN NAIROBI DAR ES SALAAM LUSAKA ADDIS ABABA
KUALA LUMPUR SINGAPORE JAKARTA HONG KONG TOKYO
DELHI BOMBAY CALCUTTA MADRAS KARACHI

© *Oxford University Press 1976*

ISBN 0 19 581000 7

*Retold by Emma Letley. Illustrated by Carol Owen. Simplified according to the language grading scheme especially compiled by D.H. Howe*

*Printed by Golden Crown Printing Co. Ltd., 3–5 Station Lane, Kowloon, Hong Kong*
*Published by Oxford University Press, News Building, North Point, Hong Kong*

# Contents

# Oxford Progressive English Readers Language Scheme

The OPER language grading scheme was especially compiled by D. H. Howe as a guide to the preparation of language teaching material for school pupils and adults learning English as a second or foreign language. The scheme provides lists of words and language structures subdivided into three grades of difficulty and meant to be used in conjunction with each other.

The items were chosen according to two main principles: first, that they are likely to have been learnt or at least encountered *before* the stage indicated; second, that they are frequently occurring and useful, necessary to express a wide range of ideas, and difficult to replace with simpler words or constructions.

Use of the scheme is intended to eliminate unnecessary difficulties of language which would otherwise hinder understanding and enjoyment.

# Introduction

*Kidnapped** is the story of the adventures of a boy who lived in Scotland in the year 1751. At the time of his adventures Scotland was divided into two parts. The geography of Scotland means that it still is in two parts, but the differences between the two were more important in the century when the hero of this story lived than they are now.

In the northern part of Scotland there were the Highlands. There were many mountains in the Highlands and groups of small islands on the west coast. These islands are the Hebrides. The Highlanders, or people who lived in the north of Scotland, were all members of different clans or large groups of families. Each clan had a chief who was the leader of his clansmen. Many of the chiefs owned a great deal of land and were extremely powerful men. The Highlanders dressed in tartan, which is a striped material of many different colours. Each clan had a different tartan.

The native language of the Highlanders was not English, but Gaelic, and many of the Highlanders spoke no English at all.

In the eighteenth century there were no large towns in the Highlands. Most of the people who lived there earned their living by farming or fishing.

In the southern part of Scotland there were the Lowlands. The hero of *Kidnapped* comes from the Lowlands. The country here was more flat and had fewer mountains than the Highlands and there were a few large towns such as Edinburgh. The people here spoke English.

In 1745, five years before *Kidnapped* begins, there was a very famous rebellion in Scotland. The Highlanders fought against the English and Lowland people. The Highlanders were led by Bonnie Prince Charlie whose followers were

*kidnap, to carry away a person by force especially so as to obtain money.

called Jacobites. At this time, George I was King of the United Kingdom, but the Jacobites thought that Bonnie Prince Charlie should have been King. King George was a Protestant. Bonnie Prince Charlie was a Roman Catholic. He was handsome and young and most Highlanders liked him much better than King George.

The King's army fought many battles against the Jacobites (the King's followers were sometimes called Whigs especially by the Highlanders). Bonnie Prince Charlie and the Jacobites won some of these battles but in the end they were defeated by the Redcoats, the name given to the King's soldiers because they wore red and white uniforms, at the Battle of Culloden. After this battle Bonnie Prince Charlie had to run away to France. Many of the Highland chiefs went with him and served the King of France. They did not dare to return to their own country because, if they had, they would have been put to death by the King.

After Culloden the English, and the Lowlanders, who were loyal to King George, were very cruel to the Highlanders. Some of the Jacobite leaders, who had not escaped to France, were shot. Others had to hide in secret places in the mountains so that the soldiers would not find them. All the Jacobite chiefs had their land taken away and they were left with very little money. Laws were made which forbade Highlanders to possess any guns or other weapons and they were forbidden to wear tartan any more.

There was one clan who did not support the Jacobites. This was the Campbell clan. They were on the side of the King. Most of the other clans, especially the Stewart clan, hated the Campbells.

# 1　The House of Shaws

I will begin my story one morning early in June 1751. I was seventeen years old and had lived all my life in the village of Essendean. My father, a schoolmaster in the village, had been dead for three weeks and it was time for me to leave home and look for work.                                                                 5

The sun was beginning to rise and the mist was lifting as I walked down the road. Mr Campbell, the minister*, was waiting for me at the garden gate. He said he would walk with me as far as the river. After a while he asked if I was sorry to leave my home.                                                              10

'If I knew where I was going,' I said, 'I would be able to give you an honest answer. I have been very happy in Essendean but I have been nowhere else. I would leave happily, however, if I thought I was going to make my fortune.'

'Well, Davie,' said Mr Campbell, 'I will tell you what you    15
are to do. Before he died your father gave me a letter. You are to take this to the House of Shaws which is near Cramond.'

I was very surprised at this. 'The House of Shaws!' I cried. 'Why did my father wish me to go to the House of Shaws?'    20

'I do not know,' replied Mr Campbell, 'but the name of the family that lives there, Balfour of Shaws, is the same as your name. It is a very old and respected house even though it has decayed a little recently.'

Then Mr Campbell gave me the letter. It was addressed to    25
Mr Ebenezer Balfour of Shaws. When I saw it I became very excited about the future. Before he left me, Mr Campbell gave me the money from the sale of my father's books, a shilling piece and a Bible. Then he returned to the village and I set off for Cramond.                                                          30

Two days after I left home, I came to the top of a hill and

*minister, a priest.

saw the city of Edinburgh below me. It seemed as if all the chimneys of the city were smoking. A flag was flying from the castle and there were many ships in the firth*.

### Strange replies to my questions

I stopped at a shepherd's* house and enquired the way to
5   Cramond, and when I reached Cramond, I asked how to get to the House of Shaws. The name of the house seemed to surprise the people I asked and I began to think there must be something strange about the place. I wanted to find out whether there was really something odd about the House of
10   Shaws and decided to change my question. I saw an old man and this time I enquired whether he knew anything about the House.

'Yes,' he replied, 'why do you ask me that?'

'Is it a big house?' I asked.

15      'It is certainly a great, huge house.'

'But,' said I, 'what can you tell me about the people who live there?'

'Are you mad?' he replied. 'There are no people there.'

'What about Mr Ebenezer?'

20      'Oh yes, he's there, but why do you want to see him?'

I replied that I hoped Mr Ebenezer might give me a job.

'What!' cried the old man. 'Take my advice and stay away from the House of Shaws!'

My next questions were answered in the same way and I
25   became very worried. Just before sunset I met a dark, cross-looking woman and asked her my usual question. She took me to the top of a hill and pointed at a huge building in the bottom of the next valley. The countryside around it was green and pleasant. There were plenty of trees and good
30   crops but the house itself seemed to be a ruin. There was no road leading up to it and no smoke coming from any of the chimneys. My heart sank. 'That is the House of Shaws!' I cried.

*firth,  narrow arm of the sea.
*shepherd,  a man who looks after sheep.

'That,' said the woman very angrily, 'is the House of Shaws and bad luck to it!' She spat on the ground. 'If you see the owner, tell him that this is the twelve hundredth and nineteenth time that Jennet Clouston has cursed him and his house, his cattle-shed and stable* and every man, guest, 5 master, wife, girl and child connected with the House!' Then she turned round with a skip and was gone.

## I approach the House of Shaws

I sat down and stared at the House of Shaws. People walked past me on their way home from work, but I was too unhappy to say 'Good evening' to them. At last the sun went 10 down and I saw a thin thread of smoke rising from one of the chimneys of the House. This comforted me a little and I set off towards the House of Shaws. After I had walked a little way I came to the main entrance. Instead of gates there were only two pieces of wood tied across the entrance with a rope 15 made out of straw. There were no walls surrounding the house and grounds, and there was no avenue. The nearer I got to the house the darker it looked. It seemed as if one part of the house had never been finished. The upper floors were not enclosed by walls and there was no glass in many of the win- 20 dows.

As it became darker, I could see a very dim light from a fire through the downstairs windows. I walked on and came to the door. I knocked.

Everything was silent. I knocked again but there was no 25 answer. I wanted to run away but then I became angry. I shouted and kicked the door. Then I heard a cough. I looked upwards and saw a man's head at one of the first floor windows. He had a gun in his hand.

'It's loaded,' he said. 30

'I have come here with a letter,' I said, 'to Mr Ebenezer Balfour of Shaws. Is he here?'

'Who is it from?' he asked.

'That does not matter,' said I.

'Well, leave it on the doorstep and go away.' 35

*stable, a building where horses are kept.

'I will not do that,' I said, 'I will deliver it to Mr Balfour. It is a letter of introduction.'

'What?' he cried. I repeated what I had said. There was a pause and then the man asked who I was.

5    'I am not ashamed of my name,' I replied. 'I am called David Balfour.'

The man's voice changed. He seemed frightened. 'Is your father dead?' I was too surprised to answer this question. 'Yes,' he continued, 'he must be dead. You are here knocking
10   on my door because he is dead. Well, I will let you in.' And he disappeared from the window.

### Ebenezer Balfour is my uncle

He opened the door and said, 'Go into the kitchen and do not touch anything.' It was dark inside the house except for the firelight but I walked to the kitchen. It was the barest
15   room I had ever seen. It was large and stone-floored with locked chests* around the walls. There were six dishes on the shelves and the table was laid for supper with a bowl of porridge*, a spoon and a cup of beer*. There was nothing else in the kitchen.

20   The man came in. He was thin and mean-looking and walked with his head and shoulders bent. It was very difficult to decide how old he was as he looked anything between fifty and seventy years old. Instead of a coat he wore a nightgown* on top of an old shirt. He had not shaved for a
25   long time. I thought he looked like an old servant who should have been left to look after the house for no wages.

'If you are hungry,' he said, 'you can eat some porridge, and you can have some water to drink if you are thirsty. I will drink the beer because it will help my cough get better.'
30   He drank the beer.

'Give me the letter.' I told him that the letter was for Mr Balfour not for him. 'I am Mr Balfour, and although you do

---

*chest, a large, strong box.
*porridge, a soft food made with grain and boiled with water.
*beer, a drink made with grain which has a sharp taste.
*nightgown, a long, loose piece of clothing worn in bed.

not seem to like me or my house or my good porridge, I am
your uncle and you are my nephew.'

I was so surprised and disappointed to learn that this man
was my uncle that I could not speak. I handed the letter to
him while he read it.                                             5

'Why did you come here?'

'I came here to deliver the letter to you,' I replied.

'I think you came because you thought I would help you,'
said he.

'Yes, sir,' I said, 'when I heard that I had rich relatives I    10
did hope they would give me a little help. But I am not a
beggar, and if you will not help me, I have plenty of friends
who will.'

'David,' he said, 'don't be angry with me. We will be good
friends.' He then asked me how long my father had been        15
dead. 'Three weeks, sir,' I replied.

'Your father was a very silent man,' continued Uncle
Ebenezer, 'he liked to keep his thoughts a secret. When he
was young he never spoke very much. Did he ever talk about
me?'                                                            20

'Until now, I did not know my father had a brother,' I
replied.

'Oh,' said my uncle, 'then I suppose you did not know
about the House of Shaws?'

'No,' I answered, 'I had not heard anything about it.'         25

My replies seemed to please him. He gave me a tap on the
shoulder and said he would take me to my bedroom.

## My first night in the house

He did not light a candle but walked into the dark passage     30
and then up the stairs. He opened the door with a key and
told me to go to bed.

'But,' I said, 'it is so dark that I cannot see the bed.'

'Well,' replied my uncle, 'there is a good moon. That will
help you to see. I do not like lights in my house because of   35
fire. Good night, David.' Before I could say anything else, he
had closed the door and locked me into the room. It was very
cold and the bed was so damp that I slept on the floor.

When there was enough daylight, I looked around the room. It was a large bedroom with three windows, and furnished in a very grand way. The furniture and curtains, though, were very old and in bad condition. Many of the window panes* were broken and the whole room was dirty and dusty. I shouted to my uncle in a loud voice. He came upstairs and let me out of the room. We had breakfast together. Again the meal was of porridge and beer.

'David,' said my uncle, 'I respect your family and I will try to help you, but you must not send letters or messages to anyone.' This made me very angry. Why did my uncle not trust me? I told him that I would leave his house.

'No, no David,' he replied, 'stay here for a day or two and I will really try to help you.'

I agreed to this and told Uncle Ebenezer that I would be very grateful for anything he could do for me. He then began to prepare to go out. He opened a chest and took out a very old blue coat and a fur hat. Suddenly he stopped his preparations. 'I can't leave you alone in the house,' he said, 'so I will have to lock you out.'

I realised that my uncle thought I was a thief. My face went red with anger. 'If you lock me out of the house,' I said, 'I will be your enemy from now on.' He thought about this for a few minutes. Then he said he would have to stay with me in the house.

### I discover something strange

The rest of the day passed fairly well. We had more porridge at midday and porridge again in the evening. It seemed as if my uncle did not eat anything else. I found a lot of books in a room near the kitchen and spent the afternoon looking at them. Then I discovered something very strange.

In one of the books I found, there was a message written in my father's clear writing. It said 'To my brother Ebenezer on his fifth birthday.' Now, I believed that Uncle Ebenezer was older than my father and that was why he had inherited* the House of Shaws when my grandfather died. But, if my

*pane, a single piece of glass in a window.
*inherit, to receive property after someone has died.

father was really younger than Ebenezer, he must have been able to write very well before he was even five years old. It seemed very strange.

I tried to forget about this but the thought kept coming back into my mind and worrying me. I asked my uncle if my $5$ father had been an especially clever little boy who could read and write well when he was very young. 'Certainly not,' replied Uncle Ebenezer, 'I was much more clever than your father. I could read as soon as he could.' My uncle's words suggested that he was younger than my father. He spoke as if $10$ he was proud that he could read at the same time as my father. He would not have said this if he was older than my father.

'Perhaps you were twins*?'

He jumped up from his stool. 'Why do you ask me that?' $15$ he shouted as he took hold of my jacket. I saw that he was shaking with fear. Then he tried to control himself and started to pretend that he was only upset because of my father's death.

I did not understand all this at all. If my father was the $20$ elder brother, why did Uncle Ebenezer own the House of Shaws? Why did my uncle seem to be afraid of me? Perhaps he was a little mad?


*The tower*

My uncle did not speak for a long time. We sat at the table and looked at each other with suspicion. The more I thought $25$ about my uncle's behaviour, the more certain I became that he had some reason to be afraid of me.

After we had our evening meal, he spoke. 'David, there is some money that I promised to give you before you were born. I would like to give it to you now. There are thirty- $30$ seven gold pieces. If you will go outside for a little while, I will go and fetch it. I will call you inside again when I have got it.' I went outside. It was a very dark night with only a few stars and I could hear the wind sighing in the distance. It seemed as if there would soon be thunder. $35$

*twins, two children with the same mother who are born at the same time.

'You can come in now,' said my uncle. I went indoors and he gave me the money. I was very surprised at this because I was certain that Uncle Ebenezer was a miser*. I was sure that he would want something from me in exchange for his
5  precious gold pieces.

A little later he looked at me out of the corner of his eye. 'Now,' he said, 'you can do something for me.' I told him I would be pleased to help him in any way I could. 'I am getting old,' he continued, 'and I would like you to give me a
10  little help in the house and garden.' I replied that I would be glad to do that. 'Well,' he said, 'we will begin at once.'

He gave me a key and asked me to go to the top of the tower at the far end of the house. I was to climb up the stairs to the top where I would find a chest. He wanted me to bring
15  this chest down with me.

'May I have a light?' I asked.

'No,' he replied, 'I have told you already that I do not like lights in my house.'

'All right,' I said, 'are the stairs safe?'
20  'They are very safe. There are no railings to hold on to, but if you keep close to the wall, you will be fine.'

The only way to get to the tower was to go outside and walk in front of the house. I went out into the night. It was very dark indeed. I walked along to the door at the bottom
25  the tower and put the key in the lock. At that moment there was a sudden flash of lightning which was so bright that it almost blinded me, and I could not see properly when it had faded away.

I opened the door. It was even darker inside the tower
30  than outside it and I had to feel my way with my hands. The walls seemed to be made of good stone and the steep steps felt quite solid under my feet. The tower had five floors. I started to climb. As I climbed higher it seemed as if the air was clearer and there was more light. I could not understand
35  this, but then there was a second flash of lightning which lit up the whole tower. There were no more steps in front of

*miser, a person who loves money for its own sake and hates spending it.

me. If I had climbed another foot, I would certainly have
been killed. I knew now that my uncle wanted to murder me.

*I frighten my uncle*

Although I was very frightened, I was so angry that I did
not have time to think about my fear. I was determined that
5   I would defeat my uncle's plan to kill me. I began to go down
the stairs very carefully. When I was about half way down,
there was a huge blast of wind which shook the tower. The
wind was followed by a very heavy shower of rain.

I reached the door at the bottom of the tower. I opened it
10  and looked out. There was another flash of lightning and I
saw my uncle standing outside his house. Then there was a
crash of thunder and he ran inside. He must have been very
frightened because he did not shut the door behind him. I
crept very quietly into the kitchen and watched what he did.
15  He did not see or hear me. He took a big bottle out of a cupboard and sat down at the table with his back towards me.
Sometimes he started to shake and sigh. Then he would take
a large mouthful of the drink in the big bottle.

I stepped closer to him and put my hand on his shoulder.
20  My uncle cried out, threw his hands up in the air and fell
to the floor in a faint. Although I was shocked by this, I
knew I must first look after myself before I looked after my
uncle. I must find a weapon to protect myself. I looked in
the chests and in one of them I found a knife. I hid this
25  under my jacket and walked over to Uncle Ebenezer.

He was lying on the floor. His face was a strange blue
colour and he seemed to have stopped breathing. I was afraid
that he might be dead. Then I got some water and splashed it
over his face. He opened his eyes. 'Sit up,' I said.
30    'Are you alive?' he cried. 'Are you alive?' Then he asked
for some medicine which I fetched for him. He looked very
sick and ill and was too weak to talk to me so I locked him in
his room and went to sleep in the kitchen.

## 2　I Go to Queensferry

It rained a great deal in the night and there was a very cold
wind the next morning. I went out of the house very early
and bathed in the river. When I came back I sat down in front
of the fire and thought about what I should do. There was no
doubt that my uncle was my enemy and wanted to kill me,　*5*
but I was too proud to run away from the House of Shaws.

I went upstairs and let my uncle out of his room. While we
were having breakfast I asked him why he had tried to kill
me. 'It was only a joke,' he replied. 'I enjoy a little fun.'
When he saw how angry I looked, he changed his manner and　*10*
promised to explain everything to me after we had finished
breakfast. I realised that he wanted time to make up an ex-
planation.

Just then we heard someone knocking at the door. I told
my uncle to sit where he was and went to open the door. In　*15*
the doorway was a young boy dressed in sailors' clothes. He
was so cold that his face looked blue. As soon as he saw me
he started to dance and sing. I asked what he wanted. He said
he had a letter for my uncle. The letter was from Captain
Hoseason who was captain of a trading ship called the　*20*
*Covenant.* He was at the Hawes Inn* in Queensferry and he
wanted to see my uncle.

'David,' said Uncle Ebenezer, 'I have some business to discuss with Captain Hoseason in Queensferry. This boy will
take me there. Come with me, and when I have finished talk-　*25*
ing to the captain, we can go and see my lawyer who is called
Mr Rankeillor. He is a man whom everyone respects. He was
also a friend of your father's. He will tell you that I will not
harm you.'

*I meet Captain Hoseason*

I thought about his suggestions and agreed to go with him.　*30*
　*inn,* a house where people can spend the night and buy food
　　and drink.

On the way to Queensferry my uncle did not say a word so I talked to the sailor boy, whose name was Ransome. He was the cabin boy* on the *Covenant*. He told me that he had worked on ships since he was nine years old but he did not
5 know exactly how old he was. While we talked he swore many times and boasted about the many wicked things he had done. He said he had stolen and lied and even murdered a man. His stories were so strange that I thought he must be lying a little. When I asked him about the ship, he said his
10 masters were cruel and that he was often beaten by the mate*, whose name was Mr Shuan. I felt very sorry for Ransome.

As soon as we reached the Hawes Inn, Ransome took us upstairs to a small room with a bed in it and a large fire made
15 of coal. A tall, dark man with a serious face was writing at a table by the chimney. Although the room was very hot he was wearing a very thick jacket and a tall cap which was pulled down over his ears. He stood up and shook hands with my uncle and they sat down at the table with a bottle in
20 front of them and a big pile of papers.

'Go outside and play for a while, David,' said Uncle Ebenezer. I did not want to leave my uncle alone with the captain because I was afraid he would make another plan to kill me. But I did want to see the sea and ships and it was too
25 hot in the captain's room, so I went outside.

I walked across the road in front of the inn and down to the beach. I had never seen the sea before and I was very excited. The smell of the sea water made me think of voyages and foreign lands. I stared at the sailors from the *Covenant*.
30 They were big, tough-looking men. Some of them wore jackets, some wore shirts and many of them had coloured handkerchiefs tied around their necks. One sailor had two small guns in his pocket and they all carried knives. I talked to one of the sailors who looked less fierce than his compan-
35 ions and he told me that the ship would sail as soon as the tide was right.

*cabin boy, a boy who works for the captain and officers of a
ship.
*mate, a ship's officer below the rank of captain.

*The House of Shaws is mine*

As I walked back to the inn, I met Ransome once more. We went inside to have a drink and something to eat. I decided to try and make friends with the landlord* and asked him if he knew Mr Rankeillor.

'Oh yes,' he replied, 'he is a very honest man. Did you    5
come here this morning with Mr Ebenezer Balfour?'

'Yes, I did,' I answered.

'Are you a relative of his?' he asked.

I replied that I was not a relative of Mr Ebenezer and that no one seemed to like him very much.    10

'He is a very wicked old man,' said the landlord, 'and there are many people who would be pleased if he was dead. He used to be a fine man, though, before the news spread about Mr Alexander.'

Mr Alexander was my father so I was very curious to hear    15
what else the landlord had to say.

'What news?'

'The news that he had been killed by his brother,' replied the landlord.

'Why should Mr Ebenezer want to kill his brother?' I asked.    20

'Because he wanted the House of Shaws.'

'Is that really true? Was Alexander the elder son?'

'Yes,' said the man. 'Alexander was the elder son and therefore he was the heir* to the House of Shaws. That is why Ebenezer wanted to kill him.'    25

---

*landlord,* the owner of an inn.
*heir,* a person who has the right by law to receive a property
   when the owner dies.

## 3  Kidnapped on the *Covenant*

I sat down and thought about my good fortune. My father
was the elder son so I was now the heir to the House of
Shaws. I could hardly believe it. Only two days before I had
had nothing and now I was the heir to a large property. I
5  would have a large house and land and a horse to ride. While I
was imagining all these pleasant things, I saw Captain Hoseason on the pier* giving orders to the sailors. He started to
walk quickly towards the inn. Then I heard my uncle calling
to me and I went and joined the two of them outside the inn.
10  The captain spoke to me with great respect.

'Sir,' he said, 'Mr Balfour has been telling me many pleasant things about you and I would like to know you better. I
wish I was in Queensferry for longer because I think we
would become good friends. We do not have much time now,
15  but come on board my ship for about half an hour and have a
drink with me.'

I wanted very much to see the inside of the ship, but I did
not want to put myself in danger. I told the captain that
Uncle Ebenezer and I had an appointment with a lawyer.

20  'Don't worry,' he said, 'Mr Balfour has already told me
about your appointment. When we have had a drink together,
and you have seen around the ship, the boat will take you
back to the pier, which is very near Mr Rankeillor's house.'

Then he leant over and whispered in my ear. 'Be careful of
25  the old fox. He wants to harm you. Come on board my ship
and I will tell you about it.'

Then Captain Hoseason put his arm through mine and continued to talk to me.

'What presents can I bring you back from America?' he
30  asked. 'Would you like some tobacco? Or the skin of a wild
animal? Or a stone pipe? Because you are a friend of Mr Balfour's, I will bring you whatever you like.'

*pier,  place where boats are tied up and passengers get off.

By this time we were beside the small boat that would take us to the *Covenant*, and I had decided to go on board with the captain. I was sure that he was my friend and did not want to harm me. I was so excited about seeing the ship that I forgot to answer the captain's questions.                    *5*

### I realise I have been kidnapped

We reached the ship and the captain helped me to climb on board. I felt a little strange because of the movement of the sea but I was delighted to be on board. Captain Hoseason told me the names and uses of many of the pieces of equipment on the deck and I was very interested to learn about the    *10* them. Suddenly I realised that my uncle was not on board the *Covenant.*

'Where is my uncle?'

Captain Hoseason looked very fierce and stern. 'That,' he said, 'is the important thing.'                    *15*

I was very frightened. I pulled myself away from the captain and ran as fast as I could to the side of the ship. Then I saw the small boat going back to the shore with my uncle in it.

'Help, help,' I shouted, 'murder!'                    *20*

When Uncle Ebenezer heard my shouts he turned round. His face was full of cruelty and terror. His face was the last thing I saw. I was pulled away from the side of the ship. I felt someone hit me very hard on the head and then I fell unconscious onto the deck.                    *25*

### I wake up

When I became conscious it was very dark and I was in great pain. My hands and feet were tied up, and I was almost made deaf by many loud, strange noises. I could hear the roar of the water, the sails blowing in the wind and the shouts of the sailors. But I was so sick and hurt that it took me quite a    *30* long time to realise where I was. I was lying in the hold* of the *Covenant* and a gale* was blowing. As soon as I had decided where I was, I went to sleep. When I woke up I could

*hold, the part of a ship, at the very bottom, where cargo is kept.
*gale, a very strong wind.

hear the same noises and, this time, I could also feel the ship swaying from side to side. I felt very seasick.

For some time (I do not know how long) I lay in the hold of the ship. I never knew what time it was, and it was so dark
5   that I could not tell the difference between night and day. At last I went back to sleep. I was woken up by a small, green-eyed man who came and shone a light on my face.

'Well,' he said, 'how are you feeling?'

I replied with a cry. He understood that I was in great pain
10  and he began to wash the wound on my head and put a bandage on it.

'Would you like some meat?'

'No,' I replied, 'I feel too ill to eat meat.'

He gave me some brandy* and water and went away.
15  The next time he came to see me I was half asleep. I no longer felt seasick but my limbs ached and the ropes which tied my hands and feet felt as if they were burning me. I thought I had a fever. Captain Hoseason came down the ladder to where I lay. Mr Riach spoke to him.
20  'Now, sir,' he said, 'you can see that the boy has a fever. He cannot eat anything and he has been down here for a long time lying in the dark. He will not recover if he stays here. We must take him to the forecastle*.'

This made the captain very angry. He told the green-eyed
25  man (whose name was Mr Riach) that he wanted me to stay where I was.

'I think you have been paid to murder the boy,' said Mr Riach, who was a little drunk.

The captain looked very frightened when he heard this.
30  'Do you think he will die if he stays here?' he asked.

'Yes,' said Mr Riach.

'Very well, then,' said the captain, 'you had better take him up to the forecastle.'

While the two men had been talking I had said nothing,
35  but I had learned two things from their conversation: first that Mr Riach was drunk and second that he was my friend. As Captain Hoseason climbed up the ladder, Mr Riach looked

*brandy,  a strong drink.
*forecastle,  the part of the ship where the sailors live and sleep.

at him and then made a very low bow as if he was laughing at him.

## Imprisoned in the forecastle

Five minutes later, the ropes around my hands and feet were cut and I was carried upstairs on a man's back. The man put me down on a bunk* and covered me with blankets. I _5_ went straight to sleep. When I woke up, I looked around the forecastle. It was a big place with many bunks. Some of the sailors were asleep. Others were sitting and smoking. It was a calm day and the sun shone brightly through the windows. I had been in darkness for such a long time that I was delighted _10_ to lie in the sunlight.

I was kept a prisoner for many days in the forecastle. I began to feel better and to learn something about my companions. Like most sailors they were rough men. Some of them had sailed with pirates*. Others had run away from the king's _15_ ships and would be punished with death if they were caught. But, in spite of these things, they were very kind to me. They talked to me and even returned most of my money which they had shared amongst themselves. I was very pleased to have this, and hoped that it would be useful to me in the new _20_ land where I was going. The *Covenant* was sailing to the Carolinas in America, and my uncle had wanted me to go there to be sold as a slave. The sailors also told me about the two mates. They said that Mr Riach was only kind when he was drunk, and Mr Shuan was always kind except when he was _25_ drunk.

One day, when Mr Riach had been drinking and seemed to be in a good temper, I told him about Uncle Ebenezer and the House of Shaws and he said he would try to help me. He promised to get me paper and pens so that I could write to _30_ Mr Campbell and Mr Rankeillor and tell them what had happened to me.

All this time the weather had been very stormy and the sea was very rough. The sailors had to work very hard and I often

*bunk, a narrow bed fixed to the wall.
*pirates, robbers who steal from ships.

heard them quarrelling with each other. Because it was so stormy, the window in the forecastle had to be kept shut. The only light in the place came from a lamp which hung from a beam. I was not allowed to go on deck and I became
5  very bored with my life in the forecastle and impatient for a change. A change came sooner than I expected.

*I start to work*

One night, at about eleven o'clock, I heard the sailors whispering to each other. They were saying, 'Shuan has murdered him at last.' There was no need for them to tell me who they
10  were speaking about. I knew it was Ransome. Captain Hoseason came into the forecastle. To my surprise he walked straight up to me and spoke to me very kindly.

'We want you to work in the roundhouse*,' he said. 'You are to change places with Ransome.'
15  As he spoke, two sailors appeared in the doorway carrying Ransome in their arms. I could see his face in the light from the lamp. It was very white and he seemed to be smiling a horrible smile.

'Go on to the deck at once,' said Captain Hoseason to me.
20  I ran quickly up the ladder on to the deck. The sea was rough and the *Covenant* was moving from side to side. Then I saw the sunset. I was very surprised at this because it was very late for a sunset. I had been shut indoors for so long that I had no idea where we were. I even thought we might be
25  halfway across the Atlantic Ocean. In fact the *Covenant* was sailing in a northerly direction round the very top part of Scotland, where the sun sets much later than in the south.

The roundhouse where I was to work was quite large. There was a table and a bench fixed to the floor. There were
30  bunks for the captain and the two mates and cupboards along the walls. They kept their possessions in the cupboards and part of the ship's food was also stored there. There was another room underneath the roundhouse where all the best food and a supply of gunpowder* was kept. All the guns

*roundhouse,* a cabin on the deck of a ship where the captain
and mates sleep and eat.
*gunpowder,* explosive which is used in guns.

were hung up on the walls of the roundhouse, but the swords were not kept in the roundhouse. There was a small window in the side of the cabin and a skylight* to light the place during the day. At night there was always a lamp burning.

## Ransome is dead

I went into the cabin and saw Mr Shuan sitting at the table 5 with a bottle of brandy in front of him. He was a tall, strong man. He did not seem to notice me and he did not move when the captain came in after me. He just stared at the table as if he was mad. I wanted to ask the captain about Ransome. 'How is he?' I asked in a whisper. Captain Hoseason just 10 shook his head and looked very solemn. After a few minutes, Mr Riach came in. He looked at Captain Hoseason. His expression clearly told us that Ransome was dead. The three of us stared at Mr Shuan. Suddenly he got up from his chair and looked very fierce. 15

'Sit down,' roared the captain, 'you have murdered the boy.'

Mr Shuan sat down again and put his head in his hands.

'Well,' he said, 'he gave me a dirty dish to eat from.'

We looked at each other in fear. Then the captain took Mr 20 Shuan to his bed and told him to lie down and sleep. The murderer cried a little but he took off his boots and obeyed.

'Mr Riach,' said the captain, 'Ransome's death must be kept a secret. If anyone asks us what happened to him, we must say he fell over the side of the ship and was drowned.' 25

I soon became accustomed to my duties in the roundhouse. I had to serve meals to the officers, to fetch food from the galley* and carry it to the roundhouse. If one of my three masters wanted a drink, I had to get it for him. At night I slept on a blanket on the floor between two doors. It was a 30 hard and cold place to sleep and I was often interrupted by someone coming into the roundhouse to get a drink. But in other ways my life was easy. The meals were simple and there was little work in preparing them. I ate the same food as the

*skylight, window in the roof.
*galley, the kitchen on a ship.

officers and I was allowed to share their drink if I wanted to. Because I was not yet used to the movement of the ship, I was often clumsy but the captain and Mr Riach were very patient with me. When he was in a good temper, Mr Riach
5    would talk to me and tell me many curious and interesting stories.

Mr Shuan's crime seemed to have made him mad. He was always surprised to see me in the roundhouse and did not seem to know who I was. One day he came very close to me.
10   His face was so white it looked as if he was dying.

'Were you here before?' he asked.

'No,' I replied.

'Was there a different cabin boy working in the round-house?'
15   I replied that there was.

'Ah,' he said, 'I thought so.'

Then he sat down and did not say another word.

In spite of the easy work and the kindness of the officers, I was worried about my future. Mr Riach would not allow me
20   to say any more about my story, and when I tried to tell the captain, he would not listen to a single word. I began to think that I would certainly become a slave working with negroes* on a tobacco plantation in America.

*_negro,_ member of a black-skinned race.

# 4   My First Meeting with Alan Breck Stewart

More than a week passed in which the weather was very stormy and the ship made little progress. On the ninth day the wind was so strong that we were driven as far south as Cape Wrath, very close to a dangerous piece of coast where there were a great many rocks. The ship's officers held a     5
meeting. They made a decision which I did not completely understand. I soon realised, however, that they must have agreed to sail south in the direction of the wind.

On the tenth day there was a thick, wet fog which hid one end of the ship from the other. In the afternoon I went out-     10
side on to the deck. Some of the sailors were leaning over the side of the ship. They were listening for breakers*. Although I did not know exactly why they were so frightened, I knew that there was some danger and I was very excited.

## The shipwrecked man

At about ten o'clock in the evening, just as I was serving     15
dinner to Captain Hoseason and Mr Riach, there was a very loud noise and the two men jumped up from their chairs.

'We have hit a rock,' said Mr Riach.

'No, Mr Riach,' said the captain, 'I think we have run into another ship.' They hurried on to the deck. The captain was     20
right. The *Covenant* had hit another ship in the fog. It had split down the centre and sunk straight to the bottom of the sea. All the crew had gone down with it except one man. He was holding on to the side of the ship. He pulled himself on board.     25

The captain brought the stranger into the roundhouse. He was quite a small man with an honest expression on his face, which was burnt very brown and covered with marks from smallpox*. His eyes moved quickly here and there and seemed

*breakers,* large waves which break on rocks.
*smallpox,* a serious disease which leaves marks on the skin.

to be laughing in a very gay way. He took off his coat and
put a pair of silver pistols* on the table and I saw that he also
had a sword. His manners were those of a gentleman. He
greeted Captain Hoseason very politely. I decided he was the
5   sort of man I would like to have as a friend.

The captain looked with great interest at the stranger's
clothes. They were French clothes and seemed much too
grand to wear on board a ship. He had a large hat with a
feather in it, a red waistcoat*, black velvet trousers and a
10   blue coat with silver buttons and fine lace.

Captain Hoseason said he was very sorry about the ship
that had sunk, and then he tried to find out who the stranger
was. He suggested he was a Jacobite* because of his French
clothes.

15   'I am a Highlander*,' said the stranger, 'and I am on my
way to France. A French ship was waiting for me near here
but I could not find it because of the fog. If you will take me
to France, I will pay you very well.'

'France?' said the captain. 'I can't take you there. This
20   ship is on its way to America. But I could take you to your
home on the west coast of Scotland.'

### The money-belt

Just then the captain noticed me hiding in the corner and
sent me away to get supper for the stranger. I wanted to get
back to the roundhouse to hear the rest of their conversation
25   so I hurried to the galley to get their food. When I returned I
saw that the gentleman had returned and taken a money-belt
from around his waist and put one or two guineas* on the
table. Both the men seemed to be excited.

'Give me half your money,' said the captain, 'and I will
30   help you.'

*pistol,  a small hand-gun.
*waistcoat,  a piece of clothing without sleeves which is worn
          under a coat or jacket.
*Jacobite, Highlander,  see introduction.
*guinea,  a gold coin worth just over a pound.

The Highlander put the guineas back into his money-belt and then put the belt on again under his waistcoat.

'I will give you thirty guineas if you take me to the shore anywhere on the west coast of Scotland,' he said, 'and, if you take me to Loch Linnhe, I will give you sixty guineas.'          5

Captain Hoseason and the stranger then shook hands and the bargain was made.

The stranger explained that the money which he carried was not his own. It belonged to the chief of his clan who was in France living as an exile*. I realised that the stranger          10
must also be an exile. After the Jacobite Rebellion in 1745, many Highlanders escaped to France. If they had stayed in Scotland they would have been put to death. Occasionally some of them, like this man with the belt of gold, came back to Scotland to collect money for their chiefs and to see their          15
friends. These men risked their lives when they returned home and I was very excited and interested to meet one of them.

Then the captain went away and I was left alone with the Jacobite.          20

'Are you really a Jacobite?'

'Yes, I am,' he replied, 'and I suppose you are a Whig*?' Now my family and Mr Campbell had taught me to be a Whig. They were loyal to King George and I had always believed they were right. But I did not want to annoy the          25
stranger so I replied that I was half-Jacobite and half-Whig.

'Well, Mr Half and Half,' said the gentleman, 'I am paying sixty guineas to your captain and I would like a drink.'

'I will go and get the key to the cupboard where the drink is kept,' I replied. I walked out on to the deck. There was still          30
a thick fog but the waves were calmer. Some of the sailors were standing at the side of the ship listening for breakers, but the captain and the mates were talking very quietly to each other. I listened very carefully. They were planning to murder the man with the belt of gold!          35

*exile, someone who is sent away from his own country as a
    punishment.
*Whig, see introduction.

*I decide to help the stranger*

When I heard that they were planning to murder the man with the belt of gold, I was very angry. The captain and his mates were wicked and greedy men who only wanted the stranger's money.

5      I walked up to them. 'Captain,' I said, 'the gentleman would like a drink. Please may I have the key to the cupboard?' They all turned round in surprise.

'This is our chance to get the pistols!' said Mr Riach. 'David, do you know where they are?'

10      'Yes, yes,' said Captain Hoseason, 'David knows where the pistols are kept. David is a good lad. You see, David, that Highlander is a danger to the ship and an enemy to good King George. We must protect ourselves against him.'

The captain had never been so polite to me since I came on 15 board the *Covenant,* but I did not let him see how surprised I was at his behaviour. He continued to explain the situation to me. 'You see, David, the problem is that all our guns are in the roundhouse and the Highland gentleman is in there with them. If I, or one of the mates, go into the roundhouse to 20 fetch the weapons he will suspect that we do not trust him. But a young lad like you could go and get them for us and he would suspect nothing. If you go and fetch the pistols, I will reward you when we arrive in America.'

Then Mr Riach whispered something in the captain's ear 25 which I could not hear. 'Yes, you are right, Mr Riach,' said the captain. Then he turned to me again. 'David,' he said, 'the Highland gentleman has a whole belt of gold. If you do what I ask, I promise that we will share the money with you.'

I told the captain I would do as he asked. He gave me the 30 key to the cupboard and I set off slowly to go back to the roundhouse. What was I to do? The captain and the mates were bad men and thieves too. They had kidnapped me. They had murdered poor Ransome, the cabin boy. Should I help them to carry out another murder? If I did not do as they 35 asked, however, they would probably murder me. I was still arguing with myself when I reached the roundhouse. The gentleman was sitting eating his supper. I do not know why, but I decided at once that I was on his side. I would help him.

## We plan to fight

I walked up to him and put my hand on his shoulder.

'Do you want to be killed?' He leapt to his feet and looked at me as if he was asking a question.

'They are all murderers on this ship,' I told him. 'They have already killed one boy on this voyage and now they want to murder you.'

He looked at me with curiosity.

'Will you stay with me and help me fight them?'

'I will,' I replied, 'I am not a thief or a murderer and I will help you.' Then he asked my name. I thought that a gentleman who wore such fine clothes must like grand people so I replied, 'David Balfour of Shaws'. It was the first time I had used the 'Of Shaws' part of my name, but it made the gentleman very angry.

'I have a King's name,' he said, 'I am called Alan Breck Stewart. It is a good name even although I do not have a large amount of property and land.' When he said this I realised that he had no land of his own. He was very vain and he had not liked the way I mentioned the House of Shaws.

After a little while his anger went away and we started to examine the roundhouse. Alan wanted to see if we would be safe in there and whether we would be able to defend ourselves against the captain and crew of the ship. The roundhouse was very well built and seemed to be very strong. There were two doors with strong locks and bolts. One of them was already shut and locked. I wanted to lock the other, but Alan said we should leave it open. That way our enemies would be in front of us where we could see them. Then he gave me a short sword and told me to put some gunpowder in the pistols.

'How many enemies have we on this ship?'

'Fifteen,' I replied.

   Alan whistled. It was going to be a tough fight for one man
and a young lad against fifteen strong sailors.
   'Well,' he said, 'we will just have to do our best. I will keep
watch at the door which is open. I think that is where the
5  main battle will be fought. You climb into the bunk and keep
watch at the window. If our enemies try to break in through
the window, you must shoot. I will teach you to be a good
fighter, David.'

## 5   The Battle and the Victory

It was now time for the battle. I had never fired a gun before and I felt very nervous. The captain and the mates had become impatient waiting for me to return with the pistols, and the next thing I knew was that the captain was standing at the open window. Alan pointed his sword at him. The captain's face turned red with anger. 'A sword?' he asked. 'Is that how you pay me back for my kindness to you?' 5

'Do not talk to me like that,' said Alan, 'I am a descendent of kings. Do you see this sword? This sword has killed more Whigs than you have toes on your feet. We will fight. Tell your crew to follow you. The sooner we start the battle the sooner you will feel this sword cut through your heart!' 10

The captain said nothing in reply to Alan's speech, but he gave me a very ugly look. 'I will not forget this, David,' he said. His voice made me tremble with fear. Then he went away. 15

'Now, David,' said Alan, 'prepare yourself for the fight.'

I filled the pistols with gunpowder and climbed up into my bunk to keep watch at the window. Alan stood ready at the open door. In one hand he held a sword and in the other a knife. There was no wind and it was so still that I could hear our enemies whispering to each other. Then I heard the sound of metal falling to the ground and I knew they were sharing the weapons amongst themselves. 20

I do not know if I was afraid but my heart beat very quickly like a bird's. I could not see clearly and I had to keep rubbing my eyes. I was full of despair and I wished that the battle was over. Then I tried to pray but I could not remember the words of the prayers I had been taught. 25

Suddenly there was a rush and a roar. Mr Shuan and Alan were fighting in the open doorway. 'He is the man who killed the cabin boy,' I shouted to Alan. 30

'Look out of your window,' cried Alan. I turned round to do so and I saw Alan put his sword through Mr Shuan's body. At the same time I saw five sailors running past the window with a very large pole. They were going to try to break down the door! I knew that I must shoot. 'Take that!' I shouted, and I fired a shot into the middle of the line of sailors. Then there was a scream. I had hit one of them. I fired two more shots and our enemies ran away from the roundhouse.

I looked around the place. It was full of smoke and my ears seemed to ring with the sound of the shots. Alan stood in the middle of the roundhouse. His sword was covered with blood and he looked very proud. Mr Shuan lay on the floor in front of him.

'How many men did you kill?'

'I think I hit one,' I replied, 'and I believe it was Captain Hoseason.' Alan said he had killed two. 'But,' he said, 'we have not killed enough of them yet. We are not safe. They will soon come back for another fight.'

### Our enemies return

I went back to my position at the window. My pistols were filled with gunpowder. There was nothing to do except listen and wait. Then we heard the sound of our enemies creeping towards the roundhouse. They were taking their places for the next battle. A signal sounded. The glass of the skylight was smashed. A man jumped through and landed on the floor. Before he could stand up, I shot at him. He made a dreadful sound and fell to the floor. Another foot started to come through the skylight. I quickly shot the man in the leg and he fell to the floor on top of his companion.

Suddenly Alan shouted to me for help. One of the sailors was holding him very tightly around his body and he could not move. Alan was trying to cut the sailor with his knife but the sailor would not let him go. Another sailor had joined in the fight. His sword was raised. I was sure we were now defeated. I raised my sword but there was no time to help Alan. The sailor let him go, and Alan ran into the middle of the

enemy roaring like a bull and swinging his sword from side to side. It seemed as if he wounded a man with each swing of his sword and our enemies ran away from him as fast as they could. They went on running until they reached the fore-
5 castle. We heard them run in and shut the door.

The roundhouse was in a terrible state. There were three dead men inside the cabin. Another man was dying in the doorway. But Alan and I were not wounded. We had beaten our enemies. Alan put his arms around me. 'David,' he said,
10 'you are a brave fighter, and I love you like a brother.' Then he dragged our enemies out of the roundhouse. He whistled a happy tune as he did this. He was very proud of our victory, but I was so weary that I could not breathe properly. The whole battle seemed like a bad dream. I could not believe that
15 I had killed two men. Before I could stop myself, I started to cry like a small child. Alan was very kind. He said I would feel better after some rest. He said he would keep watch for the first three hours and I must go to sleep. I lay down on the floor and went to sleep at once.

*We talk to the captain*
20 After three hours Alan woke me up and I kept watch for the next three hours. When dawn came the sea was calm and it was raining very hard. I looked out of the window and saw that we were sailing quite close to the coast of one of the Islands of the Hebrides. On one side of the ship I could see the
25 Isle of Skye and on the other, the Isle of Rum.

At about six o'clock we sat down to have breakfast. The floor was covered with broken glass and blood, which took away my hunger. But we were very happy. We had defeated our enemies and we had all the best food and drink on the
30 ship. Our enemies in the forecastle had only water.

Alan was in a very good temper. He took a knife and cut one of the silver buttons off his coat. 'My father gave me these buttons,' he said 'and I would like you to have one of them. Wherever you go, show the people this button and my
35 friends will help you.' Alan said this as if he was an emperor

who commanded huge armies. He was so vain that I almost laughed at his speech.

As soon as he had eaten his breakfast, Alan went to the captain's cupboard to look for a brush for his clothes. He took off his blue coat and brushed each mark and stain with great care. Then he removed each thread from the place where he had cut the silver button.

While he was busy doing this, Mr Riach shouted at us from the deck. He wanted to have a peaceful meeting with us. I climbed up to look out of the window. I sat beside it with a pistol in one hand.

'The captain,' said Mr Riach, 'would like to speak to your friend. They could speak to each other through the window.'

'How do we know the captain will not harm us?'

'I give you my solemn promise that he only wants to speak to your friend,' said Mr Riach.

I asked Alan his opinion of Mr Riach's request and we decided to agree to a meeting. Then Mr Riach asked for a drink. I gave him some brandy and he drank it very greedily.

After a while the captain came to the window. He looked very stern and pale. His face seemed so old that I was almost sorry I had shot his arm which was tied up with a large bandage. Alan held a pistol up to the captain's face. 'Please put that down,' said Captain Hoseason. 'I have promised that I will not hurt you.'

'I do not believe your promises,' said Alan.

'Very well, then,' said the captain, 'but we have more important things to talk about. We must not waste time arguing. My ship is in a dreadful state. You have killed so many of my sailors that there are not enough left to sail the ship, and Mr. Shuan, my first mate, is dead. I must go back at once to the Port of Glasgow and find some more sailors.'

*The bargain*

'No,' said Alan 'I will not agree to that. You made a bargain with me to take me to the west coast of Scotland and you must keep to your bargain.'

'How can I do that? There is no one on this ship who knows the coast near here and it is a rocky coast which is very dangerous for ships.'

'I will give you a choice,' said Alan. 'Either you can take me to any place which is within thirty miles of my own country of Appin and, if you cannot manage to do that, you must be a very poor sailor. Or, if you take me to Glasgow, I will tell everyone there about the fight on the *Covenant*. I will tell the people in Glasgow that you and your crew were beaten by one man and a young lad. Then everyone who hears my story will laugh at you and think you are a coward.'

The captain realised that he must agree to take Alan where he wished.

'Can you help us steer the ship?'

'I am not sure about that,' said Alan. 'I am a better soldier than sailor as I think you have already found out. But I know this coast quite well and I will try to help you guide the ship.'

'All right,' said Captain Hoseason, 'as soon as there is enough wind I will start sailing towards the coast, but there is one more thing I must ask you to promise. If we meet one of the King's ships and you are caught, you must leave me your money.'

'I will not agree to that,' said Alan. 'If you see a King's ship you must sail away from it as fast as you can. Now, I will make one more bargain with you. I know you do not have any brandy in the forecastle. We do not have any water in the roundhouse. I would like to exchange some brandy for two buckets of water.'

# 6  Alan's Story

After we had made our last bargain with the captain, we started to wash out the roundhouse. While we were doing this, the wind started to blow and the ship was able to set sail. The wind blew away the rain and the sun began to shine.

Now I must explain where we were. On the very foggy 5
day, when the *Covenant* ran into Alan's ship, we were sailing through the Little Minch. After the battle we were between the Isle of Canna and the Isle of Eriska. The quickest way to get from there to Loch Linnhe was to sail through the Sound of Mull. But the Captain had no map and he was afraid to sail 10
his ship so close to the islands. We set off, therefore, to sail west of Tiree and then along the southern coast of the Isle of Mull.

The early part of the day was very pleasant. Alan and I sat in the sunshine enjoying a pipe of the captain's excellent 15
tobacco. It was at this time that we told each other our stories. Alan also told me about the wild Highland country where we were going. As my home was in the Lowlands and I had never been to the Highlands before, I was glad to learn something about the place. 20

I told Alan about Uncle Ebenezer and how he had deceived me and persuaded me to go on board the *Covenant*. I told him, too, about the House of Shaws. Alan listened in a very kind way until I spoke of Mr Campbell, the minister of Essendean. When he heard the name he cried out and said 25
that he hated all the Campbells. I asked him why he hated them.

'I am a Stewart of Appin,' he replied, 'and for a long time the Stewarts have fought with the Campbells. They have deceived us and stolen our lands. The Campbells are cowards. 30
They have not defeated us in battles. Instead they have used tricks and lies to steal our houses and land. I am a Jacobite,

as you know, and the Campbells are on the side of King George.'

When he had recovered from his anger, Alan told me about his father. 'He was the best sword-fighter in the Highlands,'
5 he said, 'and a very handsome man. But he was not good with his money. He wasted it all and when he died, he left me with nothing. Because I had no money, I was forced to join the King's army in order to earn my living. At the Battle of Prestonpans in 1745 I changed sides. I left the King's army
10 and went to fight for Bonnie Prince Charlie.'

I knew that it was a very serious offence to run away from the King's army. If a soldier ran away, and was then caught, he was shot as a punishment. Alan continued. 'If the Red-coats catch me they will shoot me.'
15 'If it is so dangerous for you to be in Scotland, why didn't you stay in France?'

'I have been home every year since 1745,' Alan replied, 'and I wanted to see my friends and my country again. I have some business to do as well. When I get to my country I can
20 find men to come back to France with me who will serve the King of France. I can also collect rents for my chief who is called Ardshiel. He does not dare return to Scotland and is still in France. The English have taken away all his land and he has no home and no money. Once he had a whole army to
25 serve him. Now he has nothing. I have even seen him shop-ping in the market in France. That is a disgrace to his family and his clan.'

Then Alan told me that Ardshiel's tenants* had to pay their rents to King George. Many of them gave another rent
30 to their chief as well. 'Do you mean they pay two rents?' I asked.

### The Red Fox

'Yes,' replied Alan, 'the tenants love their chief and want to help him. Even the very poor people give a second rent for Ardshiel. His brother, who is called James Stewart of the

*tenant, a person who pays rent to the owner for a house or land.

Glens, collects the rents. I fetch\ the money from James Stewart and take it back to France for Ardshiel. Now the Red Fox is trying to stop James collecting the rents.'

'Who is the Red Fox?'

'Red Fox is the name we give to a man called Colin Campbell,' said Alan. 'He is the enemy of the Stewarts and works for the King. He hates Ardshiel. He is called Red Fox because he has red hair and is very cunning like a fox.' 5

Then Alan explained that the Red Fox worked for the King as agent for the land in Appin. This meant that he tried to rent the farms and houses to people who were on the King's side. But he had not been able to do this because the Stewarts had offered him a better price. 10

'Well, Alan,' I said, 'although I am not a Jacobite I am pleased that the Red Fox has been defeated.' 15

'The Red Fox has not been defeated,' said Alan. 'He will never be really beaten until he is dead. But one day he will not be able to escape from my revenge.'

I told Alan that it was wicked to talk about revenge in this way. This, however, made him very angry, and he told me I 20 was talking like a Campbell. I decided to change the subject. I asked him how he dared to travel around Scotland when there were so many Campbells and soldiers in his country. How did he manage not to be arrested?

'It is quite easy,' he replied. 'If there is a guard on one road 25 I take another road. There is plenty of heather* for me to hide in and I have many friends with houses where I can spend the night. It is much easier now than it was in 1746. Then there were soldiers everywhere and it was very difficult to escape from them. But now the English think the High- 30 landers are peaceful. Many of the chiefs are abroad in exile. Those that are still in Scotland are forbidden to have weapons so they are not very dangerous to the English.'

Alan stopped talking. He sat very still for a long time and did not say one word. He looked very sad. 35

*heather,   a plant with purple flowers which grows all over the
            hills in Scotland.

During our conversation I learned other things about Alan Breck. He was very skilful in all kinds of music and he was quite a famous Gaelic poet. He was a good soldier, an excellent sword-fighter and he liked fishing. All his faults could be
5 seen on his face. I knew them all now. The worst were his love of quarrelling and his vanity.

# 7   The Shipwreck

In the middle of the night the captain woke us up. 'The ship is in great danger,' he said. 'Can you come and steer her?' He looked very worried. Alan and I walked out on to the deck. The wind was blowing very hard and it was extremely cold. The moon was shining very brightly. We were sailing around   *5* the south-west corner of the Island of Mull and there were dangerous rocks all around the ship. Suddenly we heard a loud, roaring noise and saw water rising from the sea. It looked like a fountain. The captain asked what it was.

'It is the sea breaking on a reef\*,' said Alan.   *10*

'Look over there,' said the captain. 'There is another reef'.

'Yes,' said Alan, 'we must be near the Torran Rocks. There are ten miles of rocks. I think we should sail closer to the land.'

The captain gave orders to sail nearer the coast. As we   *15* came nearer to the land, it seemed as if there were reefs all around us. Once we almost hit one. Alan looked very white and frightened. Although he was a brave soldier he was afraid of the sea. 'I do not want to die like this,' he said.

At last we were round the Isle of Iona. Mr Riach, who was   *20* keeping watch for rocks from the top of the mast\*, told us that the sea in front of the ship was clear and there were no more rocks. 'You were right,' said Captain Hoseason to Alan, 'and I will remember your good advice.'

### The ship is driven against the rocks

Just then a strong current rose up and drove the ship on to   *25* a reef which we had not seen. The current was so strong that everyone on the deck was knocked down and Mr Riach almost fell off the mast. Again and again the *Covenant* was driven against the reef. We could hear the sides of the ship splitting against the rocks. Mr Riach and some of the sailors   *30*

\**reef,* a chain of rocks near the surface of the water.
\**mast,* a straight pole to which a ship's sails are attached.

tried to prepare the skiff* and lower it into the sea. But this
was not easy because the sea was very rough and the skiff was
full of heavy cargo. I went to help them take the cargo out of
the boat. The captain did not help us at all. He just stood
5    groaning each time his ship hit the reef. He loved the *Covenant* as if the ship was his wife and child and he could not bear
to see it smashed to pieces. Most of the sailors were wounded
but Captain Hoseason was much more unhappy about the
ship itself.
10    At last the skiff was ready to go into the sea. Then there
was a shout of 'Hold on!' A huge wave swept over the ship
and I was thrown into the sea. I went down under the water
and swallowed a great deal. This happened many times and I

*skiff,* a small, light boat which can be rowed by one person.

was driven further and further from the ship. Then I found that I was holding on to a piece of wood and the sea was calm. I tried to shout and wave to the men on the ship but I was too far away. They could not hear me. There seemed to be a small island a little way away. I knew I must try and     5
swim to the shore.

Although I had never learned to swim I held on to the piece of wood and kicked my legs. It was very hard work but after an hour I reached the shore. There was a small sandy beach and it seemed the most lonely place I had ever seen.     10

*The little island*

I stepped on to the shore. It was half past twelve in the morning and it was very cold. I dared not sit down because I was afraid I might freeze to death. Instead I took off my shoes and walked with bare feet on the sand. Everything was very quiet. There was no sound of men or animals. The only     15
noise was the sea breaking on the reefs.

As soon as dawn came I put on my shoes and climbed a hill. It was not easy to climb because the side of the hill was covered with large rocks and I had to jump from one to another. When I reached the top I looked out to sea but I     20
could not see the *Covenant* or the skiff. The ship must have sunk to the bottom of the sea.

My clothes were wet and I was by this time very hungry. I realised that I must find a house and some food so I began to walk along the coast. After I had walked a little way I saw     25
that I was on a very small island which was separated from the Island of Mull by a narrow strip of sea. There were no houses or people on this little island so I tried to walk across the sea to Mull. I walked into the sea at the place where the distance seemed the narrowest. The water was too deep for     30
me. Then I remembered the piece of wood which I had left behind on the shore. I walked back to the shore but the piece of wood was a long way away floating on the sea. I could not reach it. I was so cold and disappointed that I sat down and cried. I would have to stay on the small island until someone     35

came to rescue me. There was no sunshine to dry my clothes
and the rain started to pour down.

The time I spent on this island was the most unhappy part
of all my adventures. I had no food and nothing in my poc-
5   kets except money and Alan's silver button. It rained without
stopping for two days and I was full of despair.

On the first day I looked for shell fish to eat and I found
plenty on the rocks nearby. I was so hungry that I ate a lot of
them. Although they were cold and raw they seemed delici-
10  ous. However, as soon as I had eaten my first meal, I felt very
sick. I shivered and had to lie down. My second meal was
more successful. This time the fish did not make me ill and I
felt a little stronger.

On the second day I walked all over the island. It was all
15  the same. Everywhere was rocky and lonely with only sea
birds living there. But I had one piece of luck. I discovered a
very small hut like a pigs' hut which fishermen used when
they came to the island. Although the roof had fallen to the
ground and the hut gave me little shelter, it was a good place
20  for food. All around the hut there were rocks with many
shell fish. And, if I looked out of it, I could see smoke rising
from the houses of the Island of Mull. This comforted me a
little and I felt less lonely. But no one came to rescue me.

### I see two fishermen

I woke up on the third day. The rain had stopped and later
25  the sun came out. I lay down on the top of a rock to dry myself. Suddenly I saw a small boat with a brown sail. There
were two fishermen in it and it was quite close to my island. I
shouted to the fishermen, but they did not stop. They just
laughed, called back to me in Gaelic and sailed on. I could
30  not believe that they would not rescue me. I ran along the
shore shouting and waving my arms, but it was no good. I
was very angry with them and could not understand why
they would not help me.

I sat down to eat a little food and then went to sleep. In
35  the morning I saw a boat coming towards the island. Perhaps

it was the fishermen coming to get me? As the boat came
nearer I saw it was the same one that I had seen the day
before with the same two men in it. When we were close
enough to speak to each other, one of the fishermen stood up
and made a long speech to me. I told him that I did not speak    5
Gaelic. This seemed to make him very angry so I supposed
that he must be speaking in English. He spoke again. I listened very carefully, and this time I understood the word
'tide' and saw him pointing towards the Island of Mull.

'Do you mean that when the tide is out I can walk across    10
to Mull?' I asked.

'Yes, yes,' said the fisherman and he laughed very loudly as
if he thought it was all a big joke.

I ran in the direction he had pointed and came to the narrow strip of water. But now there was no water there. The    15
little island was joined to the land. It was only an island at
high tide.

## 8   The Boy with the Silver Button

I walked across to Mull. There were no roads to be seen and
the ground was soft and wet. I walked towards the smoke I
had seen from Erraid (I learned later that this was the name
of the little island). After a long time I saw a house in the
5   bottom of a small valley. It was a long, low house with a roof
made of turf. There was a little hill in front of it where an old
man sat smoking his pipe in the evening sun. He spoke a little
English and told me that the *Covenant* had sunk, but that the
sailors had swum to the shore. They had stopped at his house
10   for some food the day before.

    'Was one of them dressed like a gentleman?' I asked.

    'Yes,' said the old man, 'one of the men wore velvet trou-
sers and stockings. The others all wore sailors' trousers.'

    'Did he have a hat with a feather in it?'

15    'No,' replied the old man, 'he did not wear a hat. Are you
the lad with the silver button?'

    'Yes,' I said.

    'Well,' said the old man, 'your friend told me to look for
you. He wants you to follow him to Tororsay.'

20    I told the old man my story. He did not laugh but listened
in a kindly way. When I had finished he introduced me to his
wife. She gave me some bread and meat and her husband
prepared a drink for me. I stayed the night with these kind
Highlanders and the next morning I started to walk to Toror-
25   say.

    The country where I walked was very wild and lonely. The
fields seemed to be very small and the cattle were only the
size of donkeys. The people I saw looked very poor and there
were many beggars on the road. I lost my way several times,
30   but I could not ask the people I saw to help me because they
only spoke Gaelic.

*My strange guide*

At about eight o'clock in the evening I saw a house. I was very weary and I asked the owner to let me in. He refused and pretended that he could not speak English. Then I showed him one of my guineas and he began to speak in English at once.                                                                    5

'If you give me five shillings,' he said, 'you can spend the night in my house and tomorrow I will take you to Tororsay.' I did not sleep very well that night because I was frightened that the man might rob me. I need not have worried about this. Although my host was very poor he was not a robber. In    10 the morning he said we must go to the house of a rich man to exchange one of my guineas so that I could pay him the five shillings I owed him. The rich man's name was Hector Mac-Lean. He took my guinea and gave me twenty shillings. As my guinea was worth twenty-one shillings I realised he had    15 decided to keep one shilling for himself. Then he invited my guide and I to have dinner with his family. He made some punch* in a big bowl and my guide became so drunk that he refused to continue our journey.

We slept the night in a barn* close to the house and started    20 walking again at eight o'clock the next morning. We walked down into the valley in front of Mr LacLean's house. As we walked I noticed that my guide often stopped and looked behind him. I asked him why he did this but he would not answer and only laughed in reply.                                              25

As soon as we could not be seen from Mr MacLean's house, my guide told me that Tororsay was in front of me and that I should walk towards a nearby hill.

'Why are you telling me where to go?' I asked. 'I thought you were coming with me all the way to Tororsay.' The man,    30 who was certainly a cheat, then pretended that he could not speak English. I asked if he wanted more money.

'Give me five shillings,' he replied. I gave him two shillings which he insisted on holding in his hand. About two miles

*punch*, a drink made of wine with hot water, sugar, lemons
     and spices.
*barn*, a building where hay is kept.

further on my guide stopped again. He sat down on the
ground and took off his shoes.

'I suppose you have forgotten how to speak English again,'
I said. I lifted up my hand to hit him but then I saw that he
5   had a knife in his hand. I was so angry that I rushed towards
him, knocked the knife out of his hand and hit him in the
face. Luckily he fell down. I took his shoes and his knife and
walked on by myself.

### The blind man

After about half an hour I met a large man with a walking-
10  stick. He  seemed to be blind. He told me he was a teacher of
religion so I could trust him. In spite of this I did not like the
expression on his face which was dark and frightening. Then I
saw he had a pistol in the pocket of his coat. This surprised
me a great deal because I could not understand why a blind
15  teacher of religion needed a pistol.

He offered to take me to Tororsay. Although he was blind,
he said he knew the neighbourhood very well and would easily be able to guide me. In order to prove this to me he then
described the land around us. He was correct in every detail. I
20  was surprised at this and told him so. 'I can shoot as well,' he
said proudly, 'and if you had a pistol I would show you how
I manage it.' He did not know, of course, that I could see his
own pistol in his pocket, and I did not tell him that I also had
a pistol. Then he started to ask me questions about myself in
25  a very cunning way. He asked where my home was and whether I was rich. He said he had a gold coin which he would
like to exchange for shilling pieces. As we walked he frequently came nearer to me and each time he did this I moved
away from him. At last this made him so angry that he
30  started to swear at me in Gaelic and hit my legs with his
walking stick.

'I have a pistol too,' I said, 'and if you do not take me to
Tororsay I shall shoot you.'

When he heard this he cursed me again in Gaelic, turned
round and walked very quickly in the opposite direction.

I continued my walk. It had been a bad day for me and I had met two of the worst Highlanders that lived in Scotland. I was very glad when I reached Tororsay and found an inn where I could spend the night.

### I continue my journey

In the morning I got on the ferry from Tororsay to a place    5
called Kinlochaline which was on the mainland. The captain of the ferry boat was called MacRob. I knew that was the name of one of the other families in Alan's clan so I was very anxious to talk to him and to find out if he had seen Alan. The boat was very crowded so I was not able to speak to him    10
in private on the journey. It took a long time to get to Kinlochaline because there was no wind and there were only three oars in the boat.

When we reached the mouth of Loch Aline we saw a very sad sight. There was a huge ship full of people and on the    15
shore there were a great many more people all crying and saying goodbye. When I saw them I realised it must be a ship which was taking emigrants* to the colonies in America. As the ferry boat came near to the ship, the passengers on the ship leaned over the side crying and stretching out their    20
hands to their friends in the ferry boat. This went on for such a long time that the captain of the emigrant ship had to ask Captain MacRob to row away.

At Kinlochaline I asked Captain MacRob if he would speak to me alone. 'I am looking for someone,' I said, 'and I think    25
you may be able to help me. His name is Alan Breck Stewart.' As I spoke I offered him a shilling. This offended him a great deal.

'That is not the way one gentleman should behave to another,' he said. 'You should not offer me money. Alan Breck    30
is in France. But even if you gave me hundreds of shillings I would do nothing to harm him.' Then I showed him the silver button. His face changed.

*emigrant, someone who leaves his own country and goes to live in another.

'You should have shown me the silver button first of all,'
he said. 'If you are the boy with the silver button I have been
asked to help you. But I must tell you that you should never
say the name of Alan Breck to anyone, and you should never
5    try to bribe* a Highland gentleman.'

After this he told me where I was to go. I was to spend the
night at the inn in Kinlochaline and then start my journey to
the house of James Stewart of the Glens which was at Au-
charn. My route would take me across Morven to Ardgour on
10   the first day. On the second day I was to cross one loch at
Corran and another at Balachulish. When I got there I was to
ask the way to James Stewart's house. Then Captain Mac-
Rob gave me some advice. 'Do not speak to anyone on your
journey,' he said. 'Avoid Campbells and Redcoats. If you see
15   either, run into the bushes and hide as fast as you can.'

I walked to the inn at Kinlochaline. It was as dirty as a
shed where pigs are kept and it was full of smoke, rats and
silent Highlanders. I did not like the inn but, when it rained
very heavily, I realised I was lucky to have some shelter.

*I meet a priest*
20   I left the inn early the next morning. After I had walked a
little way I met a small man who was dressed like a priest. He
was walking very slowly and reading a book. When I saw him
I remembered the deceitful teacher of religion I had met on
Mull. But this man was a good man and not a thief. His name
25   was Mr Henderland. His home was near mine in the Lowlands
and he knew Mr Campbell, the Minister of Essendean. He had
come to the Highlands to preach to the people there. He told
me something about his work and I told him a little about
myself. I did not tell him about Alan and only said I was
30   travelling to Balachulish to meet a friend. I asked him about
the Red Fox and the Appin tenants who had to pay to rents.
'It is wonderful how they find the money,' said Mr Henderland, 'but I think they may be forced to pay the second rents
by James Stewart of the Glens, the brother of Ardshiel. There
35   is also a man called Alan Breck —'

*\*bribe,* to give someone money to persuade him to do something.

'What do you know about him?'

'He is a very bold man,' said Mr Henderland, 'and everyone knows that he helps James Stewart get the money from the tenants. Alan Breck's life is in danger already and he is a man with a very violent temper. If a tenant would not give the *5* money, I think he would be killed.'

In spite of this Mr Henderland said Alan was a fine man in many ways and very loyal to his chief.

I asked Mr Henderland what he knew about the Red Fox. He told me that the Red Fox was so angry with the people *10* who helped Ardshiel and gave him money that he was going to send the Redcoats to turn them out of their homes.

'Do you think the tenants will fight the Redcoats?' I asked.

'Well,' said Mr Henderland, 'the law says they are not allowed to have weapons but I think they probably have a few *15* guns hidden somewhere. If they have weapons I think they may fight.'

We spent the rest of the day walking and talking, and when it was evening, Mr Henderland invited me to stay the night at his house on the shore of Loch Linnhe. Before we went to *20* bed we said our prayers together and Mr Henderland gave me some money to help me on my journey.

## 9   The Red Fox Is Murdered

The next day Mr Henderland asked a fisherman to take me
across Loch Linnhe to Appin in his boat. It was about midday when I set out. It was a dark day with many clouds in
the sky and the sun shining in little patches. The sea in Loch
5   Linnhe was very deep and still with very few waves. The
mountains on either side of the Loch were very high, rough
and bare, very black and gloomy* in the shadow of the
clouds. Little rivers ran down the sides of the mountains.
Where the sun shone on them, they looked like silver threads
10   running down the mountain.

After we had been in the boat for a little while I saw a
small patch of bright red on the side of the hill. It seemed to
be moving. I asked the fisherman what this could be. He
replied that he thought it was the Redcoats marching into
15   Appin to turn the tenants out of their houses.

At last we came to a pointed piece of land at the entrance
to Loch Leven. Because this was quite near to James Stewart's house, I asked the fisherman to take me to the shore. He
put me on the shore near a wood which was called the Wood
20   of Lettermore. I was now in Alan's home country of Appin.

I was in a wood of tall trees which were growing on the
steep side of a mountain that leaned over the loch. There
were many small paths and there was a road through the
middle of the wood by the edge of which there was a spring.
25   I sat down by the spring, ate some bread which Mr Henderland had given me and thought about my plans.

My mind was full of doubts. What should I do? Was it right
to go and find Alan Breck? He was an exile and he might
even be a murderer. Perhaps it would be more sensible to
30   walk back to the Lowlands on my own? While I was thinking
about these things I suddenly heard the sound of men and
horses coming through the wood. Then I saw four travellers.

*gloomy,  dark and sad-looking.

The path in this part of the wood was so narrow that they had to walk in a line, one in front of the other, leading their horses behind them. The first man was large with red hair. He used his hat as if it was a fan and seemed to be extremely hot. The second traveller had black clothes and a white wig*. I    5
decided he must be a lawyer because of his clothes and wig. The next man was a servant. He was plainly dressed in tartan. Later I found out that it was the tartan of the Campbell clan. The fourth man I recognised as a sheriff's officer*.

## I see the Red Fox's murder

As soon as I saw these men I decided that I would go and    10
find Alan. When the first man came up to me I asked him how to get to James Stewart's house. He stopped and looked at me in a very strange way.

'Why do you want to go there?' he asked in surprise. Then I realised that I was speaking to the Red Fox.    15

'If you had asked me how to get to James Stewart's house on any other day, I would have told you. But today . . . '

He did not finish his sentence for just then there was a shot from further up the road. The Red Fox fell to the ground. He looked very frightened and his voice seemed to    20
tremble.

'Look after yourselves, I am dead,' he said to his followers. He tried to look for the wound made by the bullet but he could not open the buttons on his coat. He gave a sigh, his head rolled over on to his shoulder and he was dead.    25

The lawyer did not say anything but his face was very white with fear. The sheriff's officer ran quickly through the wood to hurry the soldiers who were on their way to Letter-more. The servant started to cry like a young child.

I looked at the side of the hill and saw a man running away    30
very fast. He was a big man dressed in a black coat with metal buttons and he carried a gun. I ran quickly up the hill shouting as I ran, 'The murderer! the murderer! There he is! I can see him!'

*wig, a covering of false hair for the head which is worn by lawyers.
*sheriff, the king's chief officer in an area or neighbourhood. The sheriff's officer works for the sheriff.

When the murderer heard my voice he looked behind him and began to run even faster. The hill was very steep and he had to run over very rocky ground. Then he disappeared and I did not see him again.

I went on running. Suddenly I heard a voice shouting at me and telling me to stop running. I looked down the hill and saw the lawyer and the sheriff's officer standing in the road. On the left of them I saw a group of Redcoats walking out of the wood.

'Why do you want me to come back?' I shouted. 'Why don't you come up the hill?'

Then I heard the lawyer shout to the Redcoats, 'Catch that boy. He has helped to murder the Red Fox. He must have been paid to stop us here.'

### I find Alan again

When I heard these words I was filled with terror. They were accusing me of murder and my life was in great danger. Some of the soldiers began to run after me while others tried to surround me. I was so frightened that I could not run. Then I heard a soft voice very close to me, 'Quick, hide here amongst the trees.' I bent down amongst the trees and saw a man holding a fishing rod. It was Alan Breck!

There was not time to speak to Alan. The soldiers started to shoot into the wood. 'Follow me,' said Alan and started to run along the side of the mountain. We ran amongst the trees. Sometimes we bent down behind very small, low hills on the side of the mountain. Sometimes we crawled on our hands and knees in the heather so that the soldiers would not see us. I was very short of breath and my heart seemed to be beating very fast. Occasionally Alan stood up straight, stopped and looked behind him. Each time he did this, we heard the shouts of the soldiers who were chasing us.

After about a quarter of an hour Alan stopped and lay down flat in the heather. 'Now,' he said, 'you must do exactly what I do, or you will be shot by the soldiers.' He turned round and began to run back to the wood from where we had

set off. This time the Redcoats did not see us. We reached the
wood and lay down panting. We had too little breath even to
speak.

'That was a hard run,' Alan said after a few minutes. I did
5   not answer him. I believed that he had helped to murder the
Red Fox. My friend was a murderer and I could not look at
his face. 'Are you still tired?' he asked.

'No,' I replied 'I am not tired and I can speak now. We
must part, Alan.'

10   Alan knew that I believed he had helped in the murder.
'David', he said 'I know nothing about the plan to murder
Red Fox. I would not murder a man in my own country
where I would bring trouble to my clan. And if I wanted to
murder a man, I would carry a gun not a fishing rod.'

15   I had to agree with this. 'Yes,' I said 'that is true enough.'
Alan then swore that he had had no part in the murder. I was
very relieved to hear this and I believed him. 'Who was the
man in the black coat?' I asked.

'I am not sure who he was,' said Alan. 'He ran past me but
20   I was bending down to tie my shoe laces and I did not see his
face clearly.'

'But Alan,' I said, 'you let the Redcoats see you and me so
that they would chase us instead of the man in the black
coat. If you did not know who he was, why did you do this?'
25   Alan would not answer this so I said no more.

*We plan to go to the Lowlands*

'We must get away from Appin as quickly as possible,' said
Alan. 'The whole of the country around here will be searched
by the soldiers for the Red Fox's murderer. Everyone will be
questioned. I must get away because I am a deserter* and will
30   be punished by death if I am caught. You must get away
because the Red Fox's friends think you were a helper in his
murder. Both our lives are in great danger.'

'But Alan,' I said, 'I am innocent. I had no part in the
murder. You know that.'

35   'No one will believe you, David,' said Alan. 'If we are
*deserter,* a person who runs away from the army.

caught we will be tried in the country of the Campbells by a
jury* of Campbells. The judge and jury will be friends of the
Red Fox, and his friends already believe you are guilty.'

This frightened me a great deal. 'Where shall we go?' I                    5
asked.

'We will go to the Lowlands,' Alan replied. His answer
comforted me a little. I wanted to return to my home in the
Lowlands and see my uncle again. 'It will be a very difficult
journey,' said Alan. 'We must get to the Lowlands without
anyone seeing us. We will not be able to get food and we will     10
have to sleep outside in the heather. But we have no other
choice. If we stay here we will be caught and charged with
murder.'

We started to crawl towards the edge of the wood.
Through the trees we could see the side of a mountain and a     15
long way away the Redcoats walking over the hill and away
from us. They had not seen us creep back to the wood. Alan
smiled as he watched. 'Now, David,' he said, 'we can sit down
and have a rest. I have a little food and drink. After we have
eaten, we will start walking to James Stewart's house where     20
we must get clothes, weapons and money.'

### Alan tells me of his adventures

While we were resting Alan told me about his adventures
since the wreck of the *Covenant*. Just before the ship sank he
had managed to climb into the skiff with Captain Hoseason,
Mr Riach and five sailors. Only they had escaped alive be-     25
cause another enormous wave had hit the ship as soon as he
had got into the skiff. This wave had drowned the wounded
sailors who were still on board the *Covenant*.

When they reached the shore Captain Hoseason told the
sailors to seize Alan and steal his gold. As the sailors started     30
to walk up behind him, Mr Riach shouted, 'Run away Alan!'
While Mr Riach fought with the other men on the shore,
Alan had run into the nearby hills. Once he stopped and

*jury, a group of people (usually 12) who decide whether a
    person who is tried in a court of law is innocent or
    guilty.

looked behind him and he saw that the sailors were fighting with each other on the shore. Each time Alan met someone, he told them that there was a shipwreck on the shore. The people were so anxious to see the wreck that they did not
5  have time to look at Alan very carefully.

He then told me how he had seen me holding on to the piece of wood in the sea and hoped that I would reach the shore safely. Because he thought I would try to find him he had told his friends to look out for the boy with the silver
10  button.

As we talked, it became very dark and it was difficult to see where we were going on the rough mountain. At about half past ten we came to the top of a hill and saw lights below us. It seemed as if the door of a house was open and the
15  light was coming from a fire and candles inside. All round the house and farm, five or six people were moving about very quickly. Each of them carried a torch.

### James Stewart of the Glens

'James must have gone mad,' said Alan. 'If we were Redcoats he would be in bad trouble. But I expect he has a man
20  keeping watch on the road for soldiers, and no Redcoat would be able to find the way we came over the mountains.' He whistled three times. At the first whistle all the torches seemed to stop moving, but at the third the hurry and movement began again. We walked down the hill and met a
25  tall, handsome man who cried out to Alan in Gaelic.

'James Stewart,' said Alan, 'please speak in English. This young gentleman does not understand Gaelic. His home is in the Lowlands and he owns a large amount of land there, but I think he will be safer in this country if I do not tell you his
30  name.'

James Stewart turned to me and said good evening. Then he spoke to Alan. 'This is a dreadful accident,' he said, 'which will bring great trouble to Appin.'

'Are you not pleased that the Red Fox is dead?' asked
35  Alan.

'No, I am afraid of what will happen to the people of
Appin,' said James, 'and, to tell you the truth, I wish the Red
Fox was alive again. Alan, Red Fox has been murdered. Who
do you think will be blamed? He was killed in our country
and our people will be punished.'                                        5

While they were talking I looked at the servants. Some of
them were on ladders. They were taking out guns and swords
from the thatched* roofs of the house and farm buildings.
Other servants carried the weapons away. A little way away I
could hear the sound of tools hitting the hard ground. I knew      10
they must be digging holes in the fields to bury the weapons
so that if the Redcoats searched the house and farm they
would not find the guns and swords. Everyone seemed very
busy and very frightened. Frequently, James would turn
away from Alan and shout more orders at his servants. They      15
were so full of fear that they did not seem to understand
what he said.

A girl came out of the house carrying a bundle. 'What is
that?' asked Alan.

'That is your French clothes,' said James. 'We must hide      20
them too. If the Redcoats search my house they will find
them and suspect that I have helped you. As you are a famous
deserter and Jacobite leader, my family, who are innocent,
will get into great trouble.'

Alan was very cross about this. 'You cannot bury my fine      25
French clothes,' he said. 'You will spoil them. I will go and
put them on.' He took the bundle from James and went into
the barn. James took me into the kitchen. At first he smiled
at me and talked to me in a friendly way, but then he became
sad and frightened. He frowned and bit his fingers and      30
seemed to have forgotten my presence. His wife sat by the
fire crying with her head in her hands. James's elder son sat
on the floor with a huge pile of papers in front of him. He
was looking through them very carefully. Some of them were
Jacobite papers. Each time he found one of these, he would      35
light it and wait for it to be completely burned.

*thatch, dried straw which is used to cover roofs.

At last James could sit still no longer and he asked if I would mind if he walked about. 'I am a bad host,' he said, 'but I can only think about this murder and how innocent people will suffer because of it.' Then he saw his son burn a
5   paper which he thought he should have kept. 'Do you want your father to be killed?' he asked. They spoke angrily to each other in Gaelic and his wife cried even more.

### James sends us away

I hated seeing the family in such sorrow and I was glad when Alan returned dressed in his French clothes. James'
10  younger son took me outside to the barn and gave me some clean clothes and some strong Highland shoes. I was pleased to have different clothes from those I had worn when I met the lawyer and the sheriff's officer in the wood of Letter-more. It would now be more difficult for the Redcoats to
15  recognise me. I went back into the kitchen. James and Alan had agreed that we must leave at once. James gave each of us some brandy, an iron pan, a sword, bullets and gunpowder. But he had no money to give us and we had very little of our own left.
20      'You must find a safe place to hide,' said James 'and send a message to me. Then I will send you money, but please leave now. Soon the Redcoats will be here to search my house. I shall be blamed for helping you. I may even be blamed for the murder,' as he said this his face turned very white. 'It
25  would be a bad thing for my family and friends if I was shot.'
Then James continued, 'If I am accused of the murder I shall have to betray you and help the Redcoats to catch you. It would be a dreadful thing to do to a friend but I must protect my own family. You must leave Scotland and your
30  young friend must go with you. Even if I am not accused of the murder, I shall have to betray him so that the Redcoats who question me will not suspect I did it. I will have to give them a description of him. I will tell them as little as possible but I will have to tell them his age and what he wore.'
35      James,' said Alan, 'surely you will not describe the clothes you have just given him?'

'No, I will not do that,' replied James. 'I will tell them he wore the same clothes he had on when the lawyer and sheriff's officer saw him.'

Alan looked at me. 'What do you think about all this?' he asked. 'Do you agree that James should betray you to the Redcoats?' I did not know what to say. I could not understand why they would not tell the truth, why they would not describe the man in the black coat who had really murdered the Red Fox to the soldiers. I asked them this. They looked at me in horror and told me not even to think of anything so dreadful. If, they said, they betrayed a Cameron to the Redcoats, the Cameron clan would never forgive the Stewarts and the two clans would become bitter enemies. I learned from this that it must have been a Cameron who murdered the Red Fox.

I realised that James would tell the soldiers about me whether or not I agreed so I thought I had better consent. 'Very well,' I said, 'blame me if you are forced to.'

After I had spoken, Mrs Stewart came and kissed me and thanked me for helping her family. She cried again and said, 'Although I do not know your name I will never forget your face and your goodness. Goodbye.'

## 10  Hiding from the Redcoats

We left James Stewart's house in the late evening. It was a warm, dark night. As it became lighter, we ran more often than we walked. At first, the country seemed to be as bare as a desert but then we passed about twenty huts and houses.
5 Each time we came to one of these, Alan left me and knocked on the door of the house or spoke at the window to the people who lived there. He did this to spread the news of the Red Fox's death. Although he was risking his life by taking the time to do this, he said it was his duty to pass the
10 news on to the other people in the neighbourhood. He felt he must warn them that the Redcoats would soon be coming to search their houses to look for the murderer.

It was daylight before we found a safe place to hide. We had reached a valley which was full of rocks, and a
15 flowing river ran through it. There were no trees and no grass and it was surrounded by huge, black mountains. Alan said the place was called the Valley of Glencoe. He frowned and looked very worried. 'We must not stay here,' he said. 'This is a place where the Redcoats are certain to search.'

20 As he spoke he started to run even faster than before. He ran down to the river to a place where there was a huge waterfall and two or three rocks in the middle of the water. He did not stop for a minute but jumped on to the rock which was nearest to him. I followed. We stood next to each
25 other on a small rock with the water rushing past us with a noise like thunder. The rock was very wet and slippery and I was afraid I might slip and fall into the river. Then I saw that we must jump even further than the first time to get to the bank on the other side. I was so frightened that I could not
30 move. Alan looked very angry. He took hold of my arm and shook me. His face was red and he stamped his foot on the rock. I covered my eyes with my hands. Alan gave me a large

drink of brandy to give me courage. 'Hang or drown. That is the choice!' he shouted as he jumped quickly to the other side of the river. I knew I must follow him. I jumped. I felt my body touch the bank but my feet slipped back into the
5     water. Alan caught hold of my collar and pulled me to the shore. Then we started to run again. I was very weary and I was glad when at last Alan stopped behind a large rock.

When I had recovered my breath a little I saw that there were really two rocks which leaned together at the top. They
10   were about twenty feet high. There were no holes in the side of the rocks for our feet and it seemed to be a very difficult climb. Alan pulled himself up to the top and then helped me climb up beside him. At the top there was a kind of hollow big enough to hide four men. It was a very good hiding place
15   because we could see a long way across the nearby country-side but, if we lay down flat, no one would be able to see us.

For a long time Alan did not speak. Then at last he smiled. 'I think we have a chance now,' he said. 'Go to sleep. I will keep watch for soldiers and I will wake you up later when
20   you have had some rest.' I lay down to sleep. It was quite comfortable and I was very tired. The last thing I heard before I went to sleep was the crying of the eagles in the distance.

### The Redcoats

Alan woke me up at about 9 o'clock in the morning. He
25   shook me roughly. 'Shh,' he said, 'you were snoring.' I did not understand why he looked so anxious and worried.

'What's wrong?' I asked. He looked over the edge of the rock and made a signal to me to do the same.

It was not full daylight. There were no clouds and it was
30   very hot. I could see the valley very clearly. About half a mile up the river there was a camp of Redcoats. A big fire was blazing and some of them were cooking. On the top of a nearby rock there was a soldier keeping water. There were many other soldiers all along the side of the river. Where the
35   land was more open and there were no trees there was a long line of soldiers on horses.

I took one quick look at them and then hid again in the hollow. 'You see what's wrong,' said Alan. 'I was afraid this would happen. They came about two hours ago. This is a very dangerous place for us to be. If they climb to the top of those hills they will be able to see us. We will only be safe *5* here if they stay down there by the side of the river.'

'What shall we do?' I asked.

'We will stay here until it is dark,' said Alan, 'and then we will try to run across the bottom of the valley without the soldiers seeing us. It will be much easier when it is dark.' *10*

We stayed there all day. The sun shone down and the rock became so hot that it was difficult to touch it without getting burnt. The little patch of earth which was cool and damp was only large enough for one of us to lie on it at a time. We took turns to lie on it. We had no water to drink so we were very *15* thirsty. All day the soldiers moved around in the valley below us. Sometimes they searched behind the rocks near the river, and sometimes they came very close to our rock.

It the afternoon it became so hot that we could bear it no longer. We were very badly burned by the sun. We climbed *20* down the side of the rock and hid in its shadow on one side. Our bodies ached so badly that we had to lie down flat on the ground. If a soldier had come near us, he would certainly have seen us. No soldier came.

After a while we felt a little stronger. By now the soldiers *25* had moved closer to the river. It was the hottest part of the afternoon and they had stopped searching the valley. The soldiers who were keeping watch were only looking at the river. Many of the other Redcoats were asleep. Alan thought it would be a good time to try to get across the valley. We *30* crawled along in the direction of the mountains.

By evening we had travelled quite a long way. Suddenly we heard the noise of water. There was a deep rushing stream. We forgot to be afraid and put our heads and shoulders straight into the cold water. Then we drank as much as we *35* could and made some food.

As soon as it was dark we set off again. At first we crawled

very carefully but soon we became braver. We stood up straight and walked at a good speed for a little way. But it soon became difficult for us to find our way up the steep mountain side and along the cliffs. There was no moon yet
5    and it was not easy to see where we were walking. Although I was not very tired now I was very frightened of falling over a rock and rolling down the side of the mountain. At last the moon rose in the sky and we could see more clearly. In the light from the moon we could see a narrow loch. Alan
10    stopped. He looked all around him to make sure that we were walking in the right direction. He seemed pleased and began to whistle many merry tunes. Some of them reminded me of my home in the Lowlands. I wished I was back in Essendean and all my adventures were over.

*Alan sends a message*
15    Before dawn on the next day we reached a split in the side of the mountain with water running through the middle. On one side there was a shallow cave in a rock. There was a pretty wood around it. The river was full of fish and there were many birds singing in the wood. From the opening of
20    the cave we could see the country of Mamore and the loch that separates Mamore from Appin. It was a pleasant place and we enjoyed the five days we spent there.

We made beds out of heather and slept inside the cave. We used Alan's coat as a blanket. Nearby we found a place where
25    no one could see us where it was safe to make a fire. We cooked hot porridge and the little fish which we caught with our hands in the river. We became rivals to see who could catch the most fish. I became very good at this which made Alan very cross as I caught more than he did.

30    When we were not catching fish or cooking, Alan taught me how to use my sword. I was not a good pupil and he became very angry and scolded me very often. Although I did not please Alan, I did learn how to hold my sword properly and to use it with more skill than before.

35    'It will be a long time before the Redcoats come here,' said

Alan. 'Before they do, we must send a message to James and
he must borrow some money for us.'

'But Alan, how can we send a message? Here we are hiding
in a lonely cave which we dare not leave. Who is to be our
messenger?' Alan thought for a while. Then he took two          5
pieces of wood from the fire and made them into a cross
which he tied with a strip of material torn from his coat.

'Could you lend me my button?' he asked. 'I know it is
strange to ask you to give back my gift but I don't want to
cut another one off my coat.' I gave him the button. He fixed   10
it to another strip of his coat and tied it around the cross.
Then he fixed a twig* of birch* and a twig of pine* on to the
cross. 'Tonight,' he said, 'I will take this cross to the house of
a good friend of mine who lives in a little village near here.
His name is John Breck. When he sees the cross he will know    15
that I am hiding near his home and that I need his help.'

'How will he know where you are?' I asked.

'He will see the pine and the birch twigs,' replied Alan 'and
he will know that I am hiding near a wood which has both
pine and birch trees growing in it. There are very, very few    20
woods that have both trees growing in them so he will come
here.'

'I see,' I said, 'that you are very clever. But why don't you
write a letter to John Breck?'

'I cannot write to him because he cannot read,' replied       25
Alan.

That night Alan took the cross and put it in his friend's
window. He was very worried when he came back to the cave
because he thought he had seen a Redcoat in the village. He
had also heard dogs barking and seen people running out of      30
their houses.

*John Breck*

Next day we saw a man walking up the mountain. He was
hiding his face behind his hand and he often looked around

---

*twig, a very small piece of wood at the end of a branch of a
    tree.
*birch and pine, two kinds of tree.

while he walked. As soon as Alan saw him he whistled, and the man started to walk towards us. Alan knew it was his friend. John Breck was dressed in rags, his face was wild and looked savage and his skin was covered with smallpox marks.

5   He seemed to be very stupid. Alan asked him to take a message to James Stewart but John Breck would not agree to this. He said he must have a letter for James or he would forget the message.

We had neither pen nor ink. Alan found a bird's feather in

10  the wood. He sharpened this and made a pen. Then he took some gunpowder and mixed it with a little water. He used this as ink. He tore a corner off his French military commission* to use as paper and sat down to write:
'Dear Kinsman*,

15  Please send money with the man who brings this to the place he knows of.'

He signed it A.S.

John Breck did not come back to the cave for three days, but on the evening of the third day, we heard the sound of

20  whistling and saw him walking towards us. He gave us news from Appin. James Stewart was in prison, he said, and the country around Appin was full of Redcoats. Alan was suspected of the murder and a reward of one hundred pounds was offered to anyone who could catch us.

25  He also brought us a note from James Stewart's wife. It was a very sad letter. With it she sent a purse with four guineas in it. It was all she could collect, she said, but she hoped it would be enough to help us. Besides the letter and the purse, she sent one of the advertisements which described

30  Alan and myself and offered the reward.

We looked at this with great interest. It described Alan as 'a small man with scars* who was about thirty-five years old and dressed in French clothes'. I was described as 'a tall.

---

*military commission,  a paper signed by the king appointing
                      an officer in the army.
*kinsman,  a relative.
*scar,  a mark left on the surface of the skin as a result of a
        disease or a wound.

strong boy of about eighteen years old, dressed in an old blue
coat and short trousers with bare legs'. Alan was pleased that
the advertisement mentioned his fine clothes and I was
relieved that it described the clothes I had left behind at
James Stewart's house. I told Alan he should take off his          *5*
French clothes so that no one would recognise him, but he
would not do so. 'I would look very foolish when I get to
France if I was wearing Highland clothes,' he said.

When he said this I once more began to wonder if I would
be safer on my own without Alan. His French clothes meant         *10*
that we would be easily recognised and then arrested. But
this was not all. If I was arrested on my own there was very
little evidence against me and I might be allowed to go free.
If I was arrested with Alan, a famous Jacobite, I would be in
bad trouble. I did not say any of these things to Alan but I       *15*
could not stop thinking them.

Alan, however, thought he was helping me and protecting
me. Once more I decided to stay with him. He thanked John
Breck and asked him for the silver button. At first John pretended that he had lost it, but Alan was very stern with him       *20*
and insisted that he return it at once. When he had returned
it, John set off back to the village and we walked in the other
direction.

## *Soldiers again*

We walked for eleven hours without stopping and early in
the morning, we saw a low piece of land, which was called        *25*
the Moor* of Rannoch. The mist was so thick that we could
not see if it was safe to go on walking. There could have been
a whole camp of soldiers on the moor and we would not have
seen them. We sat down to discuss what we should do and
agreed to wait there until the mist lifted. When it did, we saw   *30*
that the country around us was bare and that there were no
soldiers there. We could see only heather and a herd of deer
and hear only the sound of the birds.

We agreed we would have to walk towards the east. We

*\*moor,* an area of open land, especially one covered with
heather.

could not go west because that would mean we went back to Appin. To the south of the Moor of Rannoch lay Campbell country, so we could not go south. It might have been safe to go north but that would not have helped us get to the Low-
5 lands. We walked on to the moor and started to go east. There were high mountains all around us. A soldier who was keeping watch from the top of one of them could easily have seen us and we had to crawl on our stomachs. Again it was a very hot day and we had soon finished our supply of water.

10 By midday we were so weary we had to rest. We lay down in a bush of heather and Alan said he would keep watch while I slept. When I woke up Alan put a twig of heather in the ground. He told me to wake him when the shadow of the twig reached a certain place in the east. I was so sleepy and
15 tired that I could hardly keep awake. Several times I woke up suddenly and realised I had been sleeping.

The last time I woke up I saw that the sun had moved a long way in the sky. I looked at the twig of heather. I had been asleep for a long time and the shadow was a long way
20 past the place Alan had marked. I looked in front of me and saw a group of soldiers on horses coming from the south-east. They were searching the heather and coming straight towards us. I was very ashamed. Alan had trusted me to keep watch and I had gone to sleep.

25 I woke Alan. He looked at the soldiers, then at the twig and then at the sun. He frowned but he did not scold me for going to sleep. 'What shall we do?' I asked.

'We must go to that hill over there,' he said. 'It is called Ben Alder. It is a very wild, lonely mountain where there are
30 many little hollows we can hide in. If we can get there before morning we should be safe.'

'But, Alan,' I said 'we will have to go straight past the Redcoats to get to Ben Alder.'

'I know that,' he replied, 'but if we do not go that way we
35 will have to go back to Appin where we would be caught at once. Hurry up!'

As he spoke he began to run forward on his hands and

knees very quickly. He ran in and out of the low parts of the moor where we could not be seen. Some of these places had been burned and we felt a very fine dust in our faces which went into our eyes and made us cough. We were very thirsty and our wrists and knees became very painful. Sometimes we  *5* stopped behind a big bush of heather and watched the soldiers. Then we would set off again on our hands and knees. After a time I was so tired that I would happily have given up. But I was too afraid of Alan to do so. I knew how scornful he would be if I said I wanted to give up.  *10*

### The ambush*

At last, in the early part of the evening, we heard the sound of a trumpet*. We looked behind us and saw the soldiers gathering. Then we saw them make a big fire and prepare their camp for the night. They had stopped searching for us. 'Please, Alan let us sleep now,' I asked.  *15*

'We will not sleep tonight,' he said. 'We are not safe yet. We must get to Ben Alder as soon as possible. When we get there we will find a place to rest.'

'Alan,' I said, 'I would go on if I could but I cannot walk any more. I am not strong enough.' Alan said he would carry  *20* me on his back. This made me so ashamed that I had to go on. 'Very well,' I said, 'you walk first. I will follow you.'

We walked for a long time. It seemed like years. Then dawn came. We were so weary that we did not speak to each other. We looked straight in front of us and we each lifted up  *25* our feet as if they were heavy weights. We were bent over because we were so tired and we could hardly see where we were putting our feet.

We came to another hill which was covered with heather. Alan walked in front as usual. I followed a little way behind  *30* him. Suddenly there was a noise in the bushes. Three men dressed in ragged clothes jumped out of them. They knocked us down on to the ground and held knives close to our throats. We had walked into an ambush.

*ambush, a trap.
*trumpet, a musical instrument.

## 11  Cluny's Cage

I was so tired that I was almost glad that we had fallen into an ambush. I lay on the ground and looked up at the face of the man who held a knife to my throat. I heard Alan whispering to the men in Gaelic but I could not understand what
5  they were saying. Then the men took the knives away from our faces and we all sat in the heather looking at each other. 'We are very lucky,' said Alan. 'These men are our friends, clansmen of a famous Jacobite who had been hiding here for many years. His name is Cluny MacPherson. We will stay here
10  until they have told their chief about us.' I knew about Cluny. He was one of the leaders of the great rebellion in 1745. He risked his life by staying in Scotland and I had always believed that he had run away to France a long time ago.
15  'Is Cluny still here then?' I asked Alan.
'Yes, he is still here in his own country. His clansmen look after him and King George cannot harm him.' I wanted to know more about Cluny but Alan was tired and would not talk any more. He lay on his face in the heather and went to
20  sleep at once. I could hear the noise of insects everywhere. They seemed to be flying in my eyes and ears. Cluny's men talked to each other in Gaelic and I could not sleep.
At last the messenger came back. He said that Cluny would be delighted to see us and was preparing a meal. Alan was
25  very pleased about this but I felt too ill to think of food and drink. I tried to get up from the ground but my body seemed very weak. At last I managed to stand up but I could not put one foot in front of the other. I saw Alan was frowning at me. I thought it was because he was angry with me but he
30  was only thinking how tired I must be. He asked two of the men to carry me. They did this and we went through a great

many dark hollows and narrow valleys in the middle of Ben
Alder until we came to the bottom of a wood on the side of a
very steep hill. At the top of the hill there was a huge, bare
rock. Right at the top of this hill, under the rock, there was a
hut. This was Cluny's cage and it was the strangest home I          *5*
had ever seen. The whole hut was shaped like an egg. It
seemed to be half-hanging and half-standing on the hillside as
if it was a huge nest. The walls were made of tree trunks with
smaller branches and heather in between them. A tree which
grew out of the side of the hill supported the roof. Part of       *10*
the rock made the fireplace. The rock behind the hut was so
grey that the grey smoke which came from the hut could not
be seen from a distance. Inside the hut there was room for
five or six people.

This was only one of Cluny's hiding places. He had caves       *15*
and underground holes and other secret places in many parts
of the country. He had scouts who kept watch for soldiers all
over his country. If they told him the Redcoats were near
one of his hiding places he moved to another. In this way he
had managed to hide safely for five years.                        *20*

### Cluny gives us dinner

When we arrived at the cage Cluny was standing by the fire
watching a servant cooking our dinner. He was dressed simply
and wore a nightcap pulled down over his ears. He smoked a
pipe which smelled very strong and unpleasant. In spite of his
appearance he welcomed us as if he was a king who had         *25*
invited us to his palace. Alan introduced me to Cluny and we
all sat down to have a drink.

It was certainly a very strange place and Cluny was a
strange man. He had lived on his own for so long that he had
become very proud of his different homes. He had his own       *30*
seat where he would allow no one else to sit. Everything was
carefully arranged in a certain way and he did not like anything to be moved. He was very fond of cooking and, while

he talked to us, he often got up to look at the dinner he was making.

Sometimes Cluny's wife came to see him and occasionally one or two of his friends would come to the cage when it was
5   dark. Most of the time, however, he was alone and talked only to his scouts and servants. Each morning one of the servants would come and shave him and tell him all the news of his country. He was always greedy for news and asked a great many questions.

10   As soon as the meal was ready, Cluny asked us to eat. He had made a dish of meat. He squeezed a lemon over the food. 'This meal,' he said, 'is the same as the one which I gave to Bonnie Prince Charlie when he came to my cage in 1746. Let us drink to the Restoration!' We all raised our glasses and
15   drank.

### The game of cards

As soon as we had finished eating and Cluny had told us a great many stories about Bonnie Prince Charlie, he fetched a pack of cards and suggested that we should play a game. I knew he meant that we should play for money and this
20   worried me a great deal. Mr. Campbell and my father had always told me that it was wicked to play cards for money. I told Cluny I did not want to play. This made him very angry indeed and he said I was talking like a foolish Lowlander and a Whig. When I told him that I had promised my father not
25   to play cards, though, he looked less fierce, and he and Alan agreed that I should go to sleep.

I lay down at once and fell into a dreamy sleep. I thought I must be ill. Sometimes I woke up and could understand what Alan and Cluny were saying. At other times I could only hear
30   their voices and could not see where I was. Everything seemed very dark. Alan and Cluny seemed to play cards all the time I lay in bed. At first Alan won the games. Once when I woke up I saw a big pile of gold pieces on the table in front of him. It must have been about sixty guineas. Then he

began to lose. On the second day he woke me up. 'Will you give me some money?' he asked. 'Why do you want my money?' I replied. 'I only want to borrow it,' said Alan. I gave him all the money I had.

*Alan loses all my money*

On the morning of the third day I woke up feeling much better. I could see properly and I was very hungry. After breakfast I went outside into the wood. It was a grey, cool day and I sat there all morning. When I went back into the
5   hut, Alan and Cluny had stopped playing cards and were questioning one of Cluny's scouts. Cluny turned to me and spoke to me in Gaelic. I told him I did not speak Gaelic. Ever since I said I would not play cards, everything I said or did seemed to annoy Cluny. He said to me with great anger, 'My
10   scout says there are no soldiers in the south. Are you strong enough to leave my home?' I saw the cards on the table, but no gold. There was only a pile of little pieces of paper beside Cluny's place. They said that Alan owed Cluny money. He had lost more than he had. I told Cluny that I was still weak
15   and that we had very little money to go a long way. Alan looked very unhappy and worried. 'David,' he said, 'I have lost all our money.'

'Have you lost my money as well as your own?' I asked.

'Yes,' said Alan, 'I have lost your money too. You should
20   not have given it to me. I go mad when I play cards.'

'Nonsense!' said Cluny. 'I will give back your money. I will even give you double if you want it.' He began to pull the gold pieces out of his pocket but his face was very red and I knew he did not want to give it back. Alan did not
25   speak. He just looked at the floor. I asked Cluny to come outside and talk to me. I really did not know what to do. When Alan was winning the games he had kept Cluny's money. Now, when he had lost, he wanted his money back again. That seemed wrong. But Alan and I needed the money.
30   We would never be able to get to the Lowands with no money at all.

I decided to ask Cluny's advice. 'I am a young man,' I said, 'and I do not know what I should do. Would it be right for me to take your money?' He looked at me with great hatred.
35   I asked him what he would say to me if I was his son. He was silent for a few minutes.

'Mr. Balfour,' he said, 'although you have annoyed me, I think you are a good man. Take the money. That is what I would tell my son. Here it is and good luck to you!'

### The quarrel

We left Cluny's hut in the middle of the night so that no one would see us. One of Cluny's men came with us and carried our packs. He took us across Loch Erroch to another of Cluny's hiding places at the top end of Loch Rannoch. While we were walking we did not speak to each other. I was very angry with Alan for losing all our money playing cards with Cluny and he was ashamed about his loss.

Once again I thought about leaving him, but the more I thought about this the more ashamed I became. I could not leave my friend when he was in such danger. I could not say to Alan, 'You are in more danger than I am. I would be safer by myself. Continue your journey on your own. You can risk your life if you like. I will not risk mine with you.' But then I thought of Alan's behaviour at Cluny's cage. He had persuaded me to give him money when I was hardly conscious and in a great fever. That was as bad as stealing.

Although I thought these things I could not speak. I could not tell Alan I wanted to leave him but I could not tell him I forgave him either. So I said nothing.

At last Alan spoke to me. 'David,' he said, 'this is not the way two friends should behave to each other. I am sorry. I can say no more than that. If you have anything else to say, please say it now.'

'I have nothing to say,' I replied.

He seemed surprised at this. 'I know I was to blame,' he said.

'Yes, you were certainly to blame,' I said, 'but I have not scolded you about that.'

'You have not scolded me,' he said, 'but you will not speak to me. That is worse. Do you want to leave me? I do not want to stay with you if you do not want my friendship.'

This made me feel very ashamed. 'Alan Breck!' I cried. 'Do

you really think I would leave you when you are in danger? Why do you think I would be so disloyal? I have never refused to help a friend and I am not going to leave you. But there are some things which you have done which I cannot forget.'

'I know,' said Alan, 'you are thinking that you saved my life on the ship and, in exchange for this, I lost all your money. Do not make me feel more guilty about owing you so much.'

This should have made me forgive Alan but it did not. Instead I now felt guilty because I knew I was behaving badly and this made me angry. 'I have got something to say,' I said. 'You admit that you are wrong but that I have never scolded you. Now you blame me because I cannot laugh and sing in a happy way as if I was pleased that you lost all my money. Soon you will ask me to kneel down and thank you for losing it! You should think about what I feel, Alan Breck. If you thought a little more about other people you might think a little less about yourself. If a friend says nothing about an offence you should be glad about it and not make him feel guilty. You should not try to start another quarrel.'

This speech made Alan even more angry. 'Well,' he said, 'if that is what you think, there is nothing else for me to say.' We walked on in silence until we came to the hiding place at Loch Rannoch. We ate a meal and lay down to sleep without saying another word.

The next morning our guide rowed across the loch before it was light. He advised us which way we should go. He said the best and safest way to get to the Lowlands was to travel over the tops of the mountains and then come down into the Lowlands near the river Forth. Alan did not like the man's advice. 'We cannot take that route,' he said. 'If we do, we will have to walk through Glenorchy which is the country of the Campbell Clan. We should go east and walk through the country of the Atholl Stewarts. They are people of my own Clan and I would feel much safer in their country.'

Cluny's man thought Alan was wrong. He insisted that we

take his advice. He said there were many more soldiers in Stewart country than in Campbell country. 'The Redcoats will not look for you in Campbell country,' he said, 'because they would not suspect a Campbell of the Red Fox's murder. The soldiers will not be searching there. They will be in  *5* Appin and they will not expect to find you anywhere near the Campbells.'

Alan could not really argue with this and he agreed to follow the man's advice. 'Glenorchy is one of the worst places in the whole of Scotland,' he said unhappily, 'and there is noth-  *10* ing there except birds and heather and Campbells. But perhaps you are right. We will walk by your route to the Lowlands.'

## 12   The Journey to the Lowlands

We walked into the mountains and for three nights travelled
among wild hills and rivers. It rained all the time. A cold
wind blew and the mist often came down so that it was difficult for us to find our way. In the day we slept in the wet
5   heather, and at night we climbed over the rough ground as
quickly as we could. We could not light a fire because the
ground was so wet, and if we had, the soldiers might have
seen its light from far away. The only food we had was oatmeal* and a little cold meat which Cluny had given us before
10   we left the cage.

This was the worst part of our adventures since the shipwreck. I was never warm and I had a very sore throat. When I
went to sleep on the wet heather I dreamed of the most
dreadful things that had happened to me – the death of Ran-
15   some, Mr Shuan lying dead on the floor of the roundhouse
and Uncle Ebenezer standing in the rain and lightning outside
the House of Shaws. Each time I woke up I was lying in a
pool of water and the rain was pouring down.

Alan and I were still not speaking to each other. I could
20   not forgive him and we walked in silence. I should have
talked to him but I could not persuade myself to say sorry.
Although he did not say anything, Alan was kind to me. He
knew I was wet and tired and he helped me climb over the
most difficult pieces of rocky ground. I think he hoped that
25   my anger would soon pass.

### Alan starts to treat me badly

At the beginning of the third day Alan said he would carry
my pack for me. 'No,' I said, 'I can manage it very well myself, thank you.'

Alan went very red in the face. 'I will not offer to help you

*oatmeal,  grain which is used to make porridge.

again, David,' he said. 'I am not a patient man.' He said no
more but his behaviour told me what he was thinking. He
walked more quickly, whistled happy tunes and often smiled
at me in a very cunning manner. I realised he had forgiven
himself for losing all my money. In the evening the weather 5
became colder and it stopped raining. There was a strong
wind which blew away all the mist. The stars seemed very
bright. I saw that Alan was in a very good temper but the
change in weather came too late to help me. I was cold,
weary and full of pain. Alan talked quite a lot and each time 10
he said anything, he laughed at me in a scornful way. We
came to a river. 'Here is a river for you to jump, Whig!' he
said. 'I know you are very good at jumping rivers. Come on,
let's see you jump this one!'

He laughed at me in this way many times but I was too 15
miserable to say I was sorry. I knew I could not walk much
further and that soon I must lie down on the side of the
mountain and die like a sheep or fox. We walked on and I felt
worse and worse. Alan called me a Whig again. 'Mr Stewart,'
I said, 'you are older than I am and you should know how to 20
behave. It is not polite to scorn my politics in this way.' He
stopped in front of me with his head on one side and whistled
a Jacobite tune. 'It is time you stopped being so rude,' I said,
'from now on I want you to speak in a respectful way about
King George and my good friends the Campbells.' 25

'I am a Stewart . . . , ' Alan began.

'Yes,' I said, 'I know you have the name of a King, but I
have seen many people in the Highlands with that name and
I can think of nothing good to say about them.'

'That is an insult,' said Alan. 30

'I am sorry about that,' I said, 'but I have some more to
say to you. You have been chased by men on my side. Both
the Campbells and the Whigs have beaten you and now you
are running away from them. I am a Whig and a friend of the
Campbells and you should treat me as your master.' Alan 35
stood still.

'You have said something that I cannot ignore,' he said.

'No, I know that,' I said, 'and we must fight. Are you

ready?' As I spoke I held out my sword in the way Alan had taught me.

'David, David,' said Alan, 'I cannot fight you. I am much better at fighting with a sword than you are. It would be
5  murder.' He threw his sword on to the ground, 'No, no, I cannot fight with you.'

### Alan carries me

When he said this all my anger went away. I felt ill and ashamed. I wished I had not said so many foolish things but I knew that it was too late to say I was sorry. I forgot to be
10  proud. 'Alan,' I said, 'if you do not help me, I must lie down here and die. Please take me to a house where I can die more easily.'

'Can you walk?' he asked.

'No,' I replied, 'for the last hour my legs have been
15  bending under me and I have a pain in my side like a hot knife. If I die will you forgive me?'

'Don't say that,' said Alan. 'I will help you. We will walk to Balquidder and find a house where you can rest. I have friends in the village there. Take my arm.' We walked with
20  difficulty towards the village.

Alan was almost crying, 'David, I was wrong. I have not been kind to you. I forgot you were only a young lad and I could not see that you were almost dying. Please forgive me.'

'Oh, Alan, let's forget it,' I said. 'We were both to blame
25  for the quarrel. But are we almost at the village?'

'We will soon be there, but I think I had better carry you on my back.'

'You can't do that,' I said, 'I am a foot taller than you are.'

'No, no, you're not. You are only a little taller than I am. I
30  can carry you.'

'Why are you so kind to me?' I asked.

'I don't really know,' Alan said. 'I thought I liked you because we never quarrelled but now, after we have quarrelled, I like you even more.'

## A friendly house

Alan knocked at the door of the first house we came to in the village. The people who lived there came from a clan which was friendly to Alan's family. They were called MacLaren. As soon as we arrived there I went to bed and a doctor was fetched. He was a good doctor and I was young *5* and healthy so after a week I was much better. It was a month, however, before I was strong enough to travel again.

Alan would not leave me although it was very dangerous for him to stay so long in the village. During the day he hid in a hole in the side of a nearby hill under a small wood. At *10* night he came to visit me. I was always very pleased to see him. The MacLarens were very proud to have Alan as their guest and they were very kind to me.

The soldiers did not come to the house although once I saw a group of them march through the bottom of the valley *15* below the village. No one asked me why I was in the village or where I was going. This surprised me very much as many people in Balquidder knew I was at the MacLarens' house and the advertisements about us had now been printed. One of them was fixed to the bottom of my bed with a pin. Mr Mac- *20* Laren must, of course, have known who I was but I knew he would never betray me and nor would his friends in the village.

One day a man called Robin Oig came to visit me. He was a famous exile and an enemy of Alan's. He came into my *25* room with a look of great respect. 'I believe,' he said, 'that your name is Balfour.'

'Yes,' I replied, 'my name is David Balfour.'

'I have come to tell you,' he said, 'that a man called Balfour from Baith was a doctor at the battle of Prestonpans. He *30* was very kind to my brother and cured his leg which was wounded in the battle. If you are a relative of that man I shall be pleased to help in any way I can.'

This was very difficult for me to answer. I knew very little about my family. My uncle had talked about our noble rela- *35* tives but I did not know anything about this Doctor Balfour.

I told Robin Oig this. He turned round at once, without saying another word, and walked out of the room. I heard him
tell Mr MacLaren that I was 'only some fool who had no relatives and who did not even know the name of his own father.'
5   I felt his words were a disgrace to me and my family but
there was nothing I could do about it.

*The contest*

Just then Alan arrived and met Robin Oig. Both men
looked angry and proud. The stared at each other as if they
were strange dogs, looked at their swords and suggested they
10  should fight. Mr MacLaren looked very worried when he
heard this. He did not want them to fight in his house.
'Gentlemen,' he said, 'I have a much better idea. Here are my
bagpipes*. Both of you are famous pipers*. We have often
argued which of you is the best. Now we can have a contest
15  to decide.'

Alan looked at Robin. 'Are you a good piper?' he asked.
'I am an excellent piper,' Robin replied.
'That is a fine boast,' said Alan.
'Let us start the contest then,' said Robin.
20  Mr MacLaren hurried to fetch his bagpipes because he did
not want to give Alan and Robin another chance to fight.
Then he gave his guests some ham and a very good, sweet
drink. The two men sat down, one on each side of the fire.
Robin said he did not want to eat anything because he wanted
25  to save his breath for the contest, but Alan had not eaten for
ten hours and he was very hungry. 'I do not want to have any
advantage over you,' said Robin. 'Eat and drink and I will do
the same.'

When they had both eaten a little, Robin took the bag-
30  pipes and played a tune. 'Yes,' Alan said, 'you can play well.'
He took the instrument from his rival. First he played the
same tune exactly as Robin and played it. Then he played it

*bagpipes,* a musical instrument from Scotland, which has air
stored in a bag which is held under one arm and
pressed out through pipes.
*piper,* a person who plays the bagpipes.

in a different way. I enjoyed Robin's playing but I was delighted with Alan's. 'That is not bad,' said Robin, 'but you
are not very good at playing the high notes.'

Alan's face went a very bright red colour. 'You are lying,'
he cried.                                                            5

'Come on,' said Robin, do you admit you are defeated?'
He took the pipes from Alan and played the tune in the way
Alan had played it except he corrected all Alan's mistakes.
Alan's face became very angry. 'That is enough,' he said, 'you
are a good piper.' He bit his fingers. Then he got up from his    10

seat as if he was going to leave the house. Robin started to
play another tune. It was one of Alan's favourite tunes and a
special Stewart song. He sat down again, his face changed and
his anger went away as he listened to the music.

5     'Robin Oig,' he said, 'you are a great piper. I am not good
enough even to pipe in the same country as you. I cannot
fight with a man that plays the bagpipes so well.' The quarrel
was over. All night they sat in front of the fire telling stories
and piping.

### We continue our journey

10    It was now August and I was well enough to continue our
journey. The weather was warm and sunny and we thought it
would be a pleasant walk. By now we had very little money.
If we did not get to Mr Rankeillor soon, we would die of
hunger. Alan thought that the soldiers had probably stopped

15   searching for us but he said we must still be careful. 'We must
go where the Redcoats will not expect to find us,' he said.
'We will go to the old bridge of Stirling.'

The first night we went to the house of a friend of Mr Mac-
Laren's in Strathyre. On the second night we slept outside in

20   the heather. The ground was dry and it was quite warm. In
the evening we reached Allan Water and walked by the side
of it until we could see Stirling. 'You are in your own country now, David,' said Alan. 'If only we could cross the Firth
of Forth, we would be in Queensferry and our troubles

25   would be over.'

In Allan Water we made our camp on a little sandy island.
From here we could see Stirling Castle and hear the soldiers
marching in the castle grounds. In a field nearby we could see
men cutting wool from the sheep and hear them talking. We

30   had to lie down and keep quiet because we did not want anyone to see or hear us.

As soon as it began to get dark, and the men stopped working in the field, we walked across the water towards the
bridge of Stirling. The bridge was near the castle. There were

35   a few lights in the castle windows but there did not seem to

be a guard on the bridge. Everything was very still and quiet. 'Come on, Alan,' I said. 'Let's go across the bridge.'

'No,' he said, 'we must not do anything hastily. It may not be safe. We must wait until we are sure there is no guard on the bridge.' For about half an hour we lay down whispering to each other. There was no sound except the water splashing against the walls of the castle. Then an old woman started to walk across the bridge. She had a stick to help her walk and she coughed a great deal. It was so dark that we could not see her when she had passed us. 'I think she must have crossed the bridge by now,' I said.

'No,' said Alan, 'I can still hear her feet on the bridge.'

Then we heard the voice of a guard, 'Who is that?'

I think the guard must have been asleep when we arrived at the bridge. We might have got across the bridge safely while he was asleep, but now we had lost our chance. He was awake and it would be dangerous for us to try to walk across. 'This is not a safe place for us,' said Alan. 'The guard might see us.'

## We must find a boat

We started to crawl through the fields. Then we walked along a road which lead to the east. I did not understand where Alan was going and I felt very discouraged. A few minutes earlier I had been imagining myself knocking at Mr Rankeillor's door and claiming my inheritance*, and now we were still on the wrong side of the river Forth. How were we going to get across the river? 'Where are you going, Alan?' I asked.

'I am walking up the river to the place where it becomes the Firth,' he said. 'As we cannot cross the river, we will have to try to cross the Firth.'

'But, Alan,' I protested, 'there are no bridges across the Firth.'

'No,' he said, 'we will have to try to get a boat.'

'Alan, we have only got three shillings left between us. That is not enough for a boat.'

*inheritance, property or money which someone receives from a person who has died.

'David, if I cannot beg, borrow or even steal a boat, I will make one. Don't worry so much.'

We walked all night under the mountains, and in the morning, came to a little village called Limekilns. The village was
5  on the edge of the water. We could see Queensferry across the Firth on the other side. It was so close that I could even see the houses and fields and the people in them. There were many boats in the Firth but we could not cross it. Over there was Mr Rankeillor's house where great wealth was waiting for
10  me, but here I was on the wrong side of the Firth dressed in poor clothes with only three shillings in my pocket. I was wanted by the Redcoats and I was with an exile suspected of murder.

'Oh, Alan,' I said, 'over there is the end of our adventures.
15  The birds and boats can come and go across the water as often as they wish. Anyone can cross it except you and me. It is enough to break my heart!'

## 13  Alan's Plan

In Limekilns we went to a small inn and asked for some bread and cheese. We carried this outside so that we could eat it on the shore. Alan was very quiet. He was thinking very deeply about something. At last he stopped walking. 'Did you see the girl in the inn?' he asked.                                   5

'Yes,' I replied, 'I thought she was very pretty.'

'Well,' said Alan, 'that is good news, but I had hoped that she might think you were a handsome boy. I don't want her to fall in love with you. I want her to feel sorry for you. Then she will help us to get a boat. I wish you looked a little   10 paler, but I think you will be all right for my plan. We will go back to the inn.'

I laughed and followed him. 'Now, David,' said Alan, 'if you are my friend, you will do what I say. I have a plan. I am going to act a part and I would like you to help me.'         15

'Very well,' I replied, 'I will do what you tell me.'

As we came nearer to the inn, Alan told me to hold on to his arm as if I was very ill and tired and almost dying. By the time we reached the door of the inn it seemed as if he was carrying me. The girl seemed very surprised that we had come   20 back to the inn so soon, but Alan did not explain why we had done so. He helped me to sit down in a chair and asked the girl to bring me a glass of brandy. When she had brought it, Alan gave it to me in very small quantities. Then he cut my bread up into small pieces as if I was a young child. All   25 the time he was doing this, he looked at me with a very worried frown upon his face. It was not surprising that the girl felt sorry for me. She came closer to us. 'What's wrong with him?' She asked Alan.

'Wrong?' repeated Alan. 'I will tell you what's wrong with   30 him. He has walked hundreds of miles. For many weeks he has slept in wet heather. He is very ill.'

Then the girl asked if I had any friends. Alan continued,
'Yes, he has plenty of friends. He has rich relatives, a comfortable bed to sleep in, good food to eat and doctors to care
for him. But he cannot go to them. Instead he must sleep in
5  the heather like a poor beggar.'

'Why can't he go to his friends? Why must he sleep in the
heather?' she asked.

'It would not be safe to tell you that,' said Alan, 'but I will
whistle you a tune. Then you will understand.' He whistled a
10  famous Jacobite tune. At once the girl understood that we
were running away from the Redcoats.

'He is so young!' she cried.

'He is old enough to be tried and put to death,' said Alan.
When she heard these words the girl ran quickly out of the
15  room. Alan was very pleased that his plan was so successful,
but I was angry at being called a Jacobite and treated like a
child. 'Alan,' I said, 'please stop this game.'

'No, I will not,' he replied. 'If we give up now, I will be
caught and shot.'

20  The girl came back with meat and cheese. She said we need
not pay for it. While we were eating she sat at the next table
frowning and playing nervously with her dress. At last she
spoke to Alan, 'I think you talk too much,' she said. 'You
should not have told me you were Jacobites.'

25  'Perhaps you are right,' said Alan, 'but I am very careful
whom I talk to.'

'I will not betray you.'

'No, I know you will not betray us. Will you help us?'

'I cannot do that,' she replied.

30  'No,' said Alan, 'but would you help us if you could?'
She did not say a word.

*The girl agrees to help*

'Listen to me,' said Alan. 'We need a boat to take us across
the Firth during the night when no one will see us. We also
need a man to bring the boat back again to this side of the
35  Firth so that no one will suspect anyone has crossed the Firth

in the middle of the night. We have only three shillings left between us. If we do not get across the Firth we will be arrested and shot. Will you be able to lie happily in your warm bed while we are outside in the cold wind and rain? Will you be able to eat your good meat in front of a fire while this sick *5* boy lies on the side of a hill with nothing to eat or drink?' When Alan said this the girl's face became very worried. I could see that she was tempted to help us but that she did not know whether or not to believe our story. I decided to prove to her that it was true. 'Do you know Mr Rankeillor?' *10* I asked her.

'Yes, I know Mr Rankeillor, the lawyer,' she said.

'I am going to his house,' I said. 'Now you must believe that I am not a criminal. There has been a dreadful mistake and that is why my life is in danger. But I am loyal to King *15* George and I am not a Jacobite.'

When I said this, the girl's face became much more cheerful. Alan looked very cross when he heard me say I was not a Jacobite. 'I believe you,' the girl said. 'Mr Rankeillor is a good man, and you would not be going to his house if you were a *20* criminal or a Jacobite. When you have finished your meal, start walking out of the village and hide in the wood on the beach. You can trust me. I will find a way to get you across the Firth.'

We did not wait to finish our meal but set off at once to *25* the wood. It was only a small wood with a very few trees. If someone had walked past they would certainly have seen us. We hid ourselves as well as we could and waited. We stayed there all day and no one came to the wood except a piper. He was a big man with a red nose and he was very drunk. *30* He told us long stories about his hard life and he asked us a great many questions. When he went away, we were frightened that he would tell someone he had seen us in the wood and we became very impatient to get away from the place.

*The girl rows us herself*

At last darkness came. Lights went on in the houses and *35*

villages and then went out again when it was time for the
people in them to go to bed. Some time after eleven o'clock
we heard the sound of a boat. We looked at the shore and saw
the girl herself rowing towards us. She had trusted no one
5    else with our affairs and had decided to take us across the
Firth herself. When her father was asleep, she had crept out
of the inn, stolen a boat from a neighbour and come to help
us.

We did not know how to thank her for her goodness, but
10   she did not want us to thank her. She said we must hurry and
not waste time talking. Then she rowed us across the Firth
and left us on the shore not very far from Queensferry. As
soon as we had reached the shore and climbed out of the
boat, she rowed back again to the other side of the Firth. We
15   found a hiding place and lay down to sleep.

## 14   I Talk to Mr Rankeillor

The next day we agreed that Alan should stay in the country
and I should go and find Mr Rankeillor in Queensferry. I
promised to meet him in a certain place when it was dark. He
was not to move until he heard me whistling a Highland tune.

I walked to Queensferry very early in the morning. The          5
houses in the street seemed very grand and I felt foolish in
my ragged and dirty clothes. I did not dare to speak to anyone. I walked up and down the street. People looked at me in
a strange way and I became very worried. Perhaps I would
not be able to make the lawyer believe that I was telling the   10
truth? What would happen to me if he did not believe I was
really David Balfour? While I was thinking these thoughts, I
reached a very fine house. It had beautiful glass windows and
it had recently been painted. As I was looking at it with envy,
a gentleman with a kind face came out of the door. He wore    15
a wig and a pair of glasses. He asked me why I was standing
outside the door of his house. I told him that I had come to
Queensferry to discuss a matter of business and I was looking
for the house of a Mr Rankeillor. He looked very surprised. 'I
am Mr Rankeillor,' he said, 'and this is my house.'             20

'Please may I speak to you?' I asked.

'Who are you?' he said. 'I do not know your face or your
name.'

'I am David Balfour,' I replied.

'David Balfour?' he repeated in a very high voice. 'Where      25
have you been, David Balfour?'

'I have been to many strange places and had many adventures,' I said, 'but I do not want to tell you about them in the
street. Can we talk in a more private place?'

'Yes,' he said, 'I think that would be better. Come into my    30
house.'

He took me indoors and led me into a little, dusty room

which was full of books and papers. He told me to sit down.
Then he stared at my dirty clothes so that I felt ashamed.
'Now, what do you want?' he asked. 'I am very busy. Please
do not take too much of my time.'

5      'I think,' I said, 'that I am the owner of the House of
Shaws.' He took a book out of a drawer in his desk.

'You must prove that to me,' he said. 'I shall ask you some
questions.'

### Mr Rankeillor believes me

He asked me where I was born and who my father and
10   mother were. Mr Rankeillor seemed pleased with my answers.
Then he asked if I knew Captain Hoseason. 'Yes, sir,' I replied, 'I do know him. He helped my uncle to kidnap me.
The captain persuaded me to go on board the *Covenant* for a
drink, then they took me to sea. They wanted to sell me as a
15   slave in America, but the ship was wrecked.'

'Where was the *Covenant* wrecked?' asked Mr Rankeillor. I
told him that the ship sank off the south end of the Isle of
Mull.

'Yes,' he said, 'I think you are David Balfour. Now tell me
20   what you have been doing since the shipwreck. That was two
months ago. Where have you been?'

'Mr Rankeillor,' I replied, 'I cannot tell you that unless I
know that I am talking to a friend.'

'Mr Balfour,' he replied, 'I cannot be your friend until I
25   know all the facts about you. But I think you can trust me.
Although I am your uncle's lawyer, I did not know anything
about you until one day Mr Campbell came here. He wanted
to know what had happened to you and where you were. We
went to see your uncle at the House of Shaws. He said he had
30   given you some money to study abroad. He thought you had
gone to Holland. I was a little suspicious about your uncle's
story, but I could not prove that he was lying. Just then Captain Hoseason arrived at the House of Shaws. He said the
*Covenant* had been sunk and that you had been drowned. As
35   soon as he said this, I knew that Mr Ebenezer must be lying.'

'Mr Rankeillor,' I said, 'if I tell you my story, will you keep it a secret? I will have to tell you about a friend whose life is in danger. Please promise me that you will not betray him.' Mr Rankeillor gave me his promise in a very solemn manner and I began to tell him all my adventures since I had     *5* been taken on board the *Covenant* until I reached the door of his house. While I was telling my story, he sat with his eyes closed but he listened to every word. He only opened his eyes once and that was when I spoke of Alan Breck. 'Please do not tell me the names of any Highlanders,' he said. 'I am not a     *10* Jacobite. I am a lawyer and many Highlanders are wanted by the law. Luckily I am a little deaf and I did not hear the name of your friend properly. From now on we will call him Mr Thomson.'

When he said this I realised Mr Rankeillor must have heard     *15* Alan's name very clearly and have guessed I was going to mention the murder of the Red Fox. I continued my story, and each time I talked about a Highlander, I gave him a false name. I called James Stewart 'Mr Thomson's relative' and I gave the name of 'Mr Jameson' to Cluny. Colin Campbell be-     *20* came 'Mr Glen'. It seemed a foolish sort of pretence but I thought Alan would think it funny when I told him about it.

*The lawyer agrees to help me*

When I had finished telling the lawyer about my adventures, he spoke, 'Well, well you have certainly had a lot of adventures. You have told a great story and you should, I     *25* think, learn to tell it in Latin.' (Mr Rankeillor was very fond of using a great many Latin words in his conversation to show how clever he was.) 'You have travelled a long way and you have been in some very difficult situations. Mr Thomson seems to have been a very good friend to you. Even though     *30* I do not approve of his politics, I believe you are right to be so loyal to him.'

Mr Rankeillor then said he would help me. At last it seemed as if my adventures were almost over.

Mr Rankeillor invited me to have dinner with him at his     *35*

house. At once I became worried about my old and dirty
clothes, but he took me to a bedroom and gave me soap,
water and a comb. Then he laid out some clean clothes which
belonged to his son. I thought this was very kind of him. I
5  washed myself and changed my clothes and felt much better.
Then Mr Rankeillor said he would tell me about my uncle
and my father, and why they had quarrelled.

### The story of my family

   'They quarrelled,' he said, 'because of a love affair. When
they were young men, they were both very handsome and
10  they loved the same lady. She loved your father, but when
Mr Ebenezer heard about this, he pretended to be very ill. He
lay in his bed in the house with all his relatives around him.
Sometimes he would get up from his bed and go out. He
would go from one inn to another shouting about his sorrows
15  and telling anyone who would listen to him. Your father was
a good man, but sometimes he was a little weak. He could
bear Ebenezer's behaviour no longer. He said he would give
up the lady and that his brother could marry her. The lady,
however, did not want this. She did not like the two brothers
20  fighting over her in this way. She said she did not want to
marry either of them.'
   'What happened then?' I asked.
   'After a long time, your father and Mr Ebenezer made a
bargain. Although your father was the elder of the two
25  brothers and the House of Shaws should have belonged to
him when your grandfather died, he agreed that Ebenezer
should have the house. In exchange for this, they agreed that
your father should marry the lady. She agreed to this and
soon afterwards they were married. Because of this bargain,
30  your father had very little money and he and his wife lived in
a very poor way for the whole of their lives.'
   I then asked Mr Rankeillor about my own position. 'The
property is certainly yours,' he said. 'Your father was the
elder brother and you are the real heir to the House of Shaws.
35  But even although you are the real heir, your uncle will not

let you have the House of Shaws. He will fight you for it as
long as he can. You would have to go to court and fight him
for the house and land. Lawyers and court cases* are often
very expensive. What is worse is that we might have to talk
about Mr Thomson in order to prove that you were really      *5*
kidnapped. I advise you to make a bargain with Mr Ebenezer.
I think you should tell him that he can keep the house and
live there until he dies if he gives you a generous amount of
money.'

## My plan

I told Mr Rankeillor that I would think about his plan. As      *10*
I spoke I began to think of a plan of my own. 'I have a good
idea,' I said. 'We will force my uncle to admit that he had me
kidnapped. Mr Thomson will help us. We will all go to the
House of Shaws this evening.'

'But,' said the lawyer, 'that would mean I would have to      *15*
meet Mr Thomson and I do not want to meet him. I am a
lawyer. I know nothing bad about your friend. I do not *know*
that he is wanted by the law. But if I did, it would be my
duty as a lawyer to see that he was arrested. He may have
done many things against the law of this country. He may      *20*
not have told you everything about himself. He may not even
really be called Mr Thomson.' Mr Rankeillor smiled when he
said this. 'Do you still think it is a good idea that I should
meet him?' he asked.

'You must answer that question, sir,' I said.      *25*

Mr Rankeillor did not say any more then because it was
time for dinner, but I knew that he liked my plan. As soon as
we had finished dinner, he started to talk about my scheme
again. He asked me many questions about Mr Thomson and
then asked his servant to bring him a piece of paper and a      *30*
pencil. He seemed to be thinking very carefully about something. Then he started to write. When he had finished he
called for his clerk, whose name was Torrance, and said, 'I
would like you to write this clearly immediately. When you

*court case, a question which is decided in a court of law.

have copied it, please put on your hat and come with this
gentleman and me. We are going out and we will need you as
a witness.'

   As soon as the clerk had gone out of the room, I asked Mr
5  Rankeillor if he was going to try my plan. 'Yes,' he said, 'but
first I must tell you a story.' He then told me this story: 'One
day I made an appointment to meet Torrance at a certain
place in Edinburgh. We both went to the place at the time we
had agreed but we did not recognise each other. Torrance was
10 a little drunk and I had forgotten to bring my glasses with me
and I could not see him. I am so blind without my glasses that
I cannot even recognise my own clerk who has worked for me
for a very long time.' Then he laughed loudly over and over
again. I laughed too because I did not want him to think I
15 was rude. But I could not understand why he had told me
this story or why he was so very amused by it. He repeated it
several times during the afternoon, and I thought he was very
foolish to tell such a silly story so many times.

## 15   Return to the House of Shaws

In the evening we set out from Mr Rankeillor's house to go
and meet Alan at the place we had agreed. Mr Rankeillor and
I walked together and Torrance walked behind us carrying
the deed* and a large basket, which was covered with a cloth.
As we walked through the town, many people stopped and          5
bowed to the lawyer, and some of them asked his advice. At
last we had passed most of the houses and had reached the
pier and the Hawes Inn where I had first met Captain Hoseason.

I was just thinking about the captain and the Hawes Inn     10
when suddenly Mr Rankeillor put his hand in his pocket and
started to laugh. 'Oh,' he cried, 'this is very funny. I have left
my glasses at home.' As soon as he said this, I realised why he
had told me the story about Torrance and himself in Edinburgh on the day when he had forgotten his glasses. This time   15
he had left them at home on purpose so that he would talk to
Alan and Alan could help us, but he would not be able to recognise him. If anyone asked him afterwards if he had seen
Alan Breck, the Jacobite who was suspected of murder, he
would say he had not seen him. He could never swear in      20
court that he had seen Alan Breck if he had not been wearing
his glasses. It was a very clever plan. It was strange, though,
how he had managed to recognise so many people in the
street without his glasses. I believed that he could really see
quite well and was only trying to protect Alan.                 25

### Alan meets Mr Rankeillor
As soon as we had walked past the Hawes Inn, Mr Rankeillor walked behind and Torrance and I walked in front. I
whistled the Highland tune. After a while I heard Alan
whistling the same tune and he came out from behind a bush.

*deed,  a written agreement.

He seemed a little cross after his day hiding in the country. He had had a poor meal in an inn and he was very tired. When he saw my clothes and heard my plan, though, he became much more cheerful. 'That is a very good idea,' he said, 'and
5 I am the right man to help you carry it out. We must not waste any time now. I think your lawyer will be becoming impatient to see me.' I shouted to Mr Rankeillor who walked over to where we were standing. I introduced him to Alan and said, 'That is my friend Mr Thomson.'
10 'I am very pleased to meet you, Mr Thomson,' said the lawyer, 'but I must tell you that I have forgotten to bring my glasses with me. Our friend, Mr David, will tell you that I am almost blind without them, so please do not be offended if I do not recognise you tomorrow.'
15 Mr Rankeillor thought this would please Alan, but instead he was rather angry. He did not like being called Mr Thomson, and he was so vain that he thought it was an insult that the lawyer did not know he was the famous Alan Breck. 'Well, sir,' he said in a very stern voice, 'I suppose it does not matter
20 that you cannot see me properly. I thank you for telling me and for being so polite about it.'

'That is very good of you, Mr Thomson,' said Mr Rankeillor. 'Now we must continue our walk to the House of Shaws. You and I will walk together and David and Torrance will
25 walk behind us.' After he had spoken, Mr Rankeillor and Alan started to walk on. They talked to each other in whispers and Torrance and I followed behind them.

*Alan knocks on the door*

It was a long time after ten o'clock in the evening when we saw the House of Shaws. It was a dark, cool night with a
30 pleasant wind. There was no light in any part of the house. It seemed that Uncle Ebenezer had already gone to bed. We whispered to each other once more and then the lawyer and Torrance and I crept very quietly up to the house and hid behind a wall. Alan walked boldly up to the door and began
35 to knock.

For a long time Alan knocked on the door. The echoes could be heard all over the neighbourhood but no one came to answer the door. At last I heard the noise of a window being opened and I knew that my uncle must be looking out to see who was at his door. He would be able to see Alan standing on the steps but he would not be able to see us. He would think there was only one man there.                    *5*

'What do you want?' asked Uncle Ebenezer. 'It is very late to come to my house. I do not like talking to people in the middle of the night. I warn you that I have a blunderbuss*.    *10* Who are you?'

'There is no need for me to tell you my name,' said Alan, 'I have come to your house to talk to you about David.'

'David?' cried my uncle in terror.

'Do you want me to tell you his whole name?' said Alan.    *15* There was silence. Then my uncle spoke again. 'I think you had better come into my house,' he said.

'No,' Alan said, 'I will not come inside your house. I will discuss my business with you on the steps here. Please come down.' It was a long time before my uncle came to the door,    *20* but at last he appeared. He sat on the top step with his blunderbuss in his hand. He asked Alan what he wanted.

*Alan tells a false story*

Alan began to tell his story. 'As you can see,' he said, 'I am a Highland gentleman. My name is not important, but my friends and clan live near the Isle of Mull. Two months ago    *25* there was a shipwreck near there. The day after the wreck a member of my family was walking along the shore when he met a young boy who had swum to the island. My relative took this young boy to a nearby castle which is in ruins. He kept him there for almost two months and he has been a    *30* great expense to my family. When they realised that the boy came from a good family, my family asked me to come here and discuss the matter with you. If you and I do not make an agreement, you will not see the boy again.'

*blunderbuss,* a gun used to shoot at a short distance.

'Well,' said my uncle, 'I don't care if I never see the boy again. He was not a very good nephew to me and I do not wish to hear any more about him. I am not interested in him and I will not pay you a ransom\*.'

5    'Mr Balfour,' said Alan, 'this boy is your relative. Surely you will not refuse to help your brother's son? If you do not help him, everyone in the country will know about it and it will be a great disgrace to you and your family.. You will not be very popular in the neighbourhood.'

10   'I am not very popular now,' said my uncle, 'and I do not think anyone would hear about this anyway. Who is going to tell them? I will not.'

'David will tell them,' said Alan.

\**ransom,* a sum of money which is paid to someone to set a
        person free.

'David?' asked Uncle Ebenezer. 'How can he tell them if he is kept in a castle on the Isle of Mull?'

'I will explain that to you,' said Alan. 'When my family know that they will not get any ransom money for David, 5 they will not want to keep him. They will let him go and then he will be able to wander wherever he wishes.'

'I do not care,' said my uncle.

'Well,' Alan continued, 'it is clear that you do not want David back again. What do you want to happen to him? And 10 how much will you pay? Do you want us to kill the boy?'

'No, no,' cried Uncle Ebenezer, 'I do not want you to kill him. I want your family to keep him in the castle.'

'That will cost you a lot of money,' said Alan.

'The boy is my brother's son and I will have to pay you to 15 keep him. I cannot have him killed.'

'Then,' said Alan, 'we must fix the price, but first I must ask you some questions.

'Now,' he said, 'I want to agree a fair price. How much did you pay Captain Hoseason to kidnap David?'

20 'David was not kidnapped,' cried Ebenezer, 'that is a lie, a black, wicked lie!'

'Do not pretend you did not pay to have David kidnapped,' said Alan. 'Hoseason and I are partners. We share the money we make. He told me about your plan.'

25 'I paid him twenty pounds,' said my uncle, 'and he was also to have the money which he got for selling David as a slave in America.'

### Victory over Uncle Ebenezer

Uncle Ebenezer had now said all that we wanted him to say. Mr Rankeillor stepped forward and said, 'Thank you, Mr 30 Thomson. Good evening, Mr Balfour.' Then Torrance and I said good evening to my uncle. He did not say a word but just sat on the top step and looked like a man who has turned to stone. Alan took away his blunderbuss and Mr Rankeillor led him into the house. We all went into the kitchen and sat 35 and looked at my uncle. 'Now, Mr Ebenezer, do not look so unhappy,' said the lawyer, 'we will make a fair agreement with you. But before we do so, please give us the key to your cellar so that we can all share a bottle of your excellent wine.' Then he turned to me and took my hand. 'Mr David,' he said, 'I would like to congratulate* you on your good fortune. I hope you will be very happy.' Then he looked at Alan, 'Mr 5 Thomson,' he said, 'you spoke very well indeed. I would just like to know one more thing about you. Is your name James? Or Charles? Or is it perhaps George?'

Alan began to look angry. 'Why should my name be any of those three names?' 10

'Because, sir,' said Mr Rankeillor, 'you mentioned that you had a king's name. I do not think there has ever been a King Thomson so I thought you must be talking about your first name.'

Alan thought this was a great insult and he became very 15 angry. He did not answer the lawyer's questions, but walked away to the far end of the room and sat down and frowned. After a while I walked over to him and thanked him for helping me. He began to smile once more and I persuaded him to come and sit by the fire and have a drink with us. 20

We lit the fire and opened a bottle of wine. Torrance and I and Alan sat in the kitchen while my uncle and the lawyer went and discussed their business in the next room. After about an hour they came into the kitchen. They seemed to have made an agreement. My uncle was to give me a large 25 part of the income each year from the House of Shaws. He was to live there until he died and then the house and land would be mine. I was now a rich man.

That night we all slept at the House of Shaws. The others all slept very well, but I was too excited to sleep. I lay awake 30 until dawn looking at the light from the fire and thinking about the future.

*congratulate, to tell someone that you are pleased that something good has happened to him.

## 16    The End of the Story

My troubles were over but I was still worried about two
things. Alan was still in great danger. Without him I might
never have reached the House of Shaws. Somehow I must
help him escape to France. The second thing which worried
5  me was the murder of the Red Fox, and James Stewart of the
Glens. James was in prison and I knew that he was innocent.
What was I going to do about that? I decided I would go to
Mr Rankeillor's house and ask his advice about both these
matters.
10     I did this the next morning. He agreed with me about my
duty to Alan. 'You must certainly help him get to France,' he
said. 'I will give you a letter to take to my bank and they will
give you plenty of money. Give Mr Thomson as much as he
needs. If he has enough money, he will know the best way to
15  get to France.'
When we talked about the murder the lawyer advised me
not to interfere in the matter. He told me that a certain noble-
man called the Duke of Argyle was trying to take his revenge
on James Stewart of the Glens. The duke was a relative of the
20  Red Fox and he believed that James was responsible for the
murder. 'But,' said Mr Rankeillor, 'if you interfere and try to
stop his revenge, he will try to stop you from doing so. He
will have *you* tried in a Highland court with a Highland jury
and you will then be accused of the murder and punished by
25  death. If you want to protect yourself, and at the same time
help James Stewart, you must not let the Duke of Argyle
know you are doing so. I will tell you what you are to do. I
will give you a letter to take to a lawyer who will help James
Stewart. You can tell this lawyer what you know about
30  James and why you know he is innocent, but I do not think
you need mention your friend Mr Thomson.' He gave me the
two letters, one to the bank and one to the lawyer who would
help James, said goodbye and left me.

Alan and I started to walk towards Edinburgh. We walked very slowly and did not speak very often. We were both very sad because we would soon have to say goodbye. Then we talked about what we should do. We agreed that I should get Alan some money, go to a lawyer who was a Stewart of Appin and a friend of Alan's and ask him to find a ship which would take Alan to France. This lawyer would make all the arrangements for his escape, Alan said. While I was doing these things, Alan would hide nearby and we would meet once each day so that I could tell him what I had arranged.

After we had made our plans we tried to be cheerful. Alan laughed at my new clothes and I tried to make a joke of calling him 'Mr Thomson', but we were very close to tears. We came to the top of a hill above Edinburgh. I gave Alan some money. We looked at each other in silence and then said goodbye. I walked down the hill into Edinburgh until I came to the doors of the bank.

# Questions

*Chapter* 5  1. How many sailors did David and Alan kill in the battle?
2. Where did their enemies go after the battle?
3. Why did Alan give David one of his silver buttons?
4. How did Alan persuade Captain Hoseason to sail towards Appin and not go back to Glasgow?

*Chapter* 6  1. Why did Alan become angry when David spoke of Mr Campbell, the Minister?
2. Why had Alan left France and come to Scotland?
3. What else did David learn about Alan?

*Chapter* 7  1. Why was the ship in danger?
2. How did David manage to swim to the shore?
3. Why could David not get to the Island of Mull?
4. Why do you think the fishermen did not come to rescue David the first time they sailed past in their boat?

*Chapter* 8  1. Why did David and his guide have to go to Hector MacLean's house?
2. Do you think the blind man was really blind? Why do you think so?
3. Do you think he was really a teacher of religion? Why do you think so?
4. Why was David anxious to talk to the captain of the ferry?
5. Why did Mr Henderland think that Ardshiel's tenants paid a second rent?

*Chapter* 9  1. Whom did David meet walking through the wood?
2. How did he know who they were?
3. Why did they think David was part of the plan to murder the Red Fox?
4. Why did David tell Alan they must part?
5. Why did Alan say they must leave Appin at once?
6. What were James Stewart's servants doing when Alan and David arrived at his house?
7. Why were they doing this?
8. What did David agree James should do to protect himself and his family?

*Chapter  10*  1. Why did Alan stop at all the houses they passed in the hills?
2. Where did David and Alan hide?
3. Why could David and Alan not leave their hiding place for a long time?
4. Why did they think it was safe to leave it in the afternoon?
5. How did Alan send a message to John Breck?
6. What news did John Breck give them about Appin?
7. Why did David want Alan to change his clothes?
8. Why did they go east?
9. How did they tell the time?

*Chapter  11*  1. Who were the men who ambushed David and Alan?
2. Why was David so surprised that their chief was in Scotland?
3. Why was their host angry with David?
4. How did Alan lose all their money?
5. Why was David worried about taking back the money from their host?
6. Why did David and Alan quarrel?
7. Why did Cluny's man tell them to travel through the country of the Campbells?

*Chapter  12*  1. For how long did they travel over the mountains?
2. How did Alan help David to get to Balquidder?
3. What did David think was a disgrace to him and his family?
4. How did Mr MacLaren prevent Alan and Robin Oig from fighting?
5. Why did David and Alan not know there was a guard on the bridge when they first got there?
6. Why was it so difficult for them to cross the water to Queensferry?

*Chapter  13*  1. How did Alan try to persuade the girl to help them?
2. What did David say that finally made her decide to help them?

*Chapter 14*  1. What lies had Mr Ebenezer Balfour told Mr Rankeillor?
2. How had Mr Rankeillor known that they were lies?
3. Why did Mr Rankeillor not want David to tell him the real names of Alan and the other Highlanders he had met?
4. Why had David's father and his uncle quarelled?
5. What bargain had they made with each other?
6. What story did Mr Rankeillor tell David several times?

*Chapter 15*  1. Why had Mr Rankeillor told David this story?
2. How did David now know the reason?
3. Why was Mr Rankeillor's plan so clever?
4. What story did Alan tell David's uncle to explain why he had come to the House of Shaws?
5. Why do you think he told this story?
6. What did Mr Rankeillor and Mr Ebenezer Balfour agree about the House of Shaws and the income from it?

*Chapter 16*  1. What were the two matters about which David was still worried?
2. What did Mr Rankeillor tell him to do about them?

# OXFORD PROGRESSIVE ENGLISH READERS

## GRADE 1

Vocabulary restricted to 1900 head words
Illustrated partly in two and partly in full colours
One illustration every 6 pages on average

| | |
|---|---|
| The Adventures of Hang Tuah | MUBIN SHEPPARD |
| Alice's Adventures in Wonderland | LEWIS CARROLL |
| A Christmas Carol | CHARLES DICKENS |
| Don Quixote | CERVANTES |
| Great Expectations | CHARLES DICKENS |
| Gulliver's Travels | JONATHAN SWIFT |
| Islands in the Sky | ARTHUR C. CLARKE |
| Jane Eyre | CHARLOTTE BRONTË |
| Little Women | LOUISA M. ALCOTT |
| Madam White Snake | RETOLD BY BENJAMIN CHIA |
| Oliver Twist | CHARLES DICKENS |
| Plays for Malaysian Schools I | PATRICK YEOH |
| The Stone Junk | RETOLD BY D.H. HOWE |
| Stories of Shakespeare's Plays I | RETOLD BY N. KATES |
| The Tale of the Bounty | RETOLD BY H.G. WYATT |
| Tales from Tolstoy | RETOLD BY R.D. BINFIELD |
| Tales of Si Kabayan | MURTAGH MURPHY |
| The Talking Tree & Other Stories | DAVID McROBBIE |
| The Tiger of Lembah Pahit | NORMA R. YOUNGBERG |
| A Time of Darkness | SHAMUS FRAZER |
| Treasure Island | R.L. STEVENSON |

## GRADE 2

Vocabulary restricted to 2900 head words
One two-coloured illustration every 10 pages on average

| | |
|---|---|
| Around the World in Eighty Days | JULES VERNE |
| Asia Pacific Stories | MURTAGH MURPHY |
| Beau Geste | P.C. WREN |
| Chinese Tales of the Supernatural | RETOLD BY BENJAMIN CHIA |
| The Crocodile Dies Twice | SHAMUS FRAZER |
| David Copperfield | CHARLES DICKENS |
| Five Tales | OSCAR WILDE |
| Hound of the Baskervilles | SIR ARTHUR CONAN DOYLE |
| The Missing Scientist | S.F. STEVENS |
| Plays for Malaysian Schools II | PATRICK YEOH |
| Robinson Crusoe | DANIEL DEFOE |
| Seven Chinese Stories | T.J. SHERIDAN |
| Stories of Shakespeare's Plays II | RETOLD BY WYATT & FULLERTON |
| A Tale of Two Cities | CHARLES DICKENS |
| Tales of Crime & Detection | RETOLD BY G.F. WEAR |
| Two Famous English Comedies | RETOLD BY RICHARD CROFT |
| Vanity Fair | W.M. THACKERAY |

# GRADE 3

Vocabulary restricted to 3500 head words
One two-coloured illustration every 15 pages on average

| | |
|---|---|
| Animal Farm | GEORGE ORWELL |
| The Gifts & Other Stories | O. HENRY & OTHERS |
| Journey to the Centre of the Earth | JULES VERNE |
| Kidnapped | R.L. STEVENSON |
| King Solomon's Mines | RIDER HAGGARD |
| Lady Precious Stream | S.I. HSIUNG |
| The Moonstone | WILKIE COLLINS |
| A Night of Terror & Other Strange Tales | GUY DE MAUPASSANT |
| Pride and Prejudice | JANE AUSTEN |
| The Red Winds | SHAMUS FRAZER |
| Seven Stories | H.G. WELLS |
| Stories of Shakespeare's Plays III | RETOLD BY H.G. WYATT |
| Tales of Mystery & Imagination | EDGAR ALLAN POE |
| 20,000 Leagues under the Sea | JULES VERNE |
| The War of the Worlds | H.G. WELLS |
| Wuthering Heights | EMILY BRONTË |

TURRIFF ACADEMY